D0906631

GROUNDWORK GUIDES

Series Editor
Jane Springer

GROUNDWORK GUIDE

ornography
ebbie Nathan

Groundwood Books
House of Anansi Press

Toronto Berkeley

Thanks to Bobby Byrd at Cinco Puntos Press, who connected me with my wonderful editors for *Pornography* — Patsy Aldana, Jane Springer and Sarah Quinn. Thanks also to Vicki Mayer for getting me to the Adult Entertainment Expo in Las Vegas. Kudos to my children, Sophy and Willy, who provided teenaged and early-twenty-something answers to my endless questions about their (and their friends') take on porn. And thanks especially to Morten Naess, who's always with me as I work, in body, soul and mind.

Groundwood Books / House of Anansi Press
110 Spadina Avenue, Suite 801, Toronto, Ontario M5V 2K4
Distributed in the USA by Publishers Group West
1700 Fourth Street, Berkeley, CA 94710

ONTARIO ARTS COUNCIL
CONSEIL DES ARTS DE L'ONTARIO

We acknowledge for their financial support of our publishing
program the Canada Council for the Arts, the Government of
Canada through the Book Publishing Industry Development
Program (BPIDP) and the Ontario Arts Council.

Library and Archives Canada Cataloguing in Publication
Nathan, Debbie
Pornography / by Debbie Nathan
(Groundwork guides)
Includes bibliographical references and index.
ISBN-13: 978-0-88899-766-1 (bound)
ISBN-10: 0-88899-766-3 (bound)
ISBN-13: 978-0-88899-767-8 (pbk.)
ISBN-10: 0-88899-767-1 (pbk.)
1. Pornography. 2. Pornography – social aspects. I. Title. II. Series.
HQ471.N34 2007   363.4'7   C2006-906684-1

Design by Michael Solomon
Printed and bound in Canada

Contents

In memory of Ellen Willis (1941-2006), who always had her eyes open, and who knew that in order to think hard and hold our visions, we must have the right to look.

Chapter 1
Thinking About Porn

When was the first time you received an email message whose heading made you think it was from a friend, but when you opened it, you found pictures of nude people in sexual poses? When did you first type "XXX" into a search engine such as Google, then click on some of the thousands of sites that popped up?

Nowadays, sexual images are absurdly easy to find for anyone with a way into the Internet. Unless a web connection has a filter on it there is almost nothing to keep people — including minors — from entering porn sites. A 2001 study by the Henry J. Kaiser Family Foundation found that seven out of ten fifteen- to seventeen-year-olds in the United States have looked at pornography online.[1] In another survey, completed in 2004, seven in ten eighteen- to twenty-four-year-old men reported that they had visited an online porn site in the month before the study was conducted.[2]

Images are not the only porn available these days — words are everywhere, too. When this writer was in high school in the US in the late 1960s, a cheerleader was suspended for using the word "horny" at a school assembly. Today, the vocabulary in Internet chat rooms — including those for teenagers — routinely gets far more hardcore and no one bats an eye. Even when the discussion is about something besides sex, conversation often gets waylaid by unknown newcomers — maybe adults, maybe not — spouting dirty language. Meanwhile, bookstores display products like the bestseller *How to Make Love Like a Porn Star*. It's a memoir by Jenna Jameson, who has been filmed having sex in dozens of XXX-rated DVDs. Jameson's co-author is a former reporter at the highly respected *New York Times*.

There is also cable TV, with some channels showing porn late at night and others running it twenty-four hours a day. Viewers without subscriptions can make out nude bodies through the "snow" that supposedly blocks the visuals, and they can clearly hear moaning. Sex is on prime-time TV, too, in wildly popular shows such as *Sex and the City*, a US product that has also been a hit in countries like the UK and Canada. The series cheerfully promotes practices such as anal sex and sex toys. "Look," exclaims Charlotte, one of the four main characters, when she gets her first vibrator. "Oh, it's so cute!…it's pink! For girls!"[3]

And there is music. Hip-hop includes torrents of pornographic lyrics. "Conversate, sex on the first date," goes a typical song by The Notorious B.I.G. that often plays on daytime commercial radio. "Then I, whip it out, rubber no doubt/Step out, show me what you all about/Fingers in your mouth, open up your blouse/Pull your G-string down South." These days, dancing to all kinds of music involves moves that only strippers used to make in public — and not many people used to see strippers. Yet today, "exotic" dancing is so well accepted that gymnasiums in Canada, Britain, Australia and the US offer classes in "pole dancing" for women as a form of exercise. These classes resemble aerobics sessions, except that instructors tell students to "smack your butt," "touch, feel, and caress the body."[4]

Sexualized language and imagery is so widespread now that even conservative, religion-based businesses are jumping on the bandwagon in order to sell their products. Thomas Nelson, Inc. is a US-based Christian publisher with titles such as *Liberalism Is a Mental Disorder* and *Home Invasion: Protecting Your Family in a Culture That's Gone Stark Raving Mad*. But in 2006, Thomas Nelson started a new Christian imprint. It is called Naked Ink, and it will include a child-rearing guide for parents called *The Hot Mom's Handbook*.

US writer Pamela Paul has coined a word to describe what has happened to modern life. It has been "pornified," she says. Barely forty years old herself, Paul remembers that things were much tamer when she was a teenager, in the days before Internet, cable TV and the Jenna Jameson book. That was a generation ago. Now, says Paul, pornography is hurting people, including children and young adults.[5]

But is it really? Who says so? And why do they say it?

Some people who are troubled by porn claim that it makes men want to have sex outside of marriage or masturbate, which are sins against God. This reasoning comes from traditional Jewish, Christian and Muslim beliefs. It is a moral argument, and those who do not take the Bible or Qur'an literally — who don't find anything wrong with masturbation, for instance — probably will not take such arguments seriously.

Still, many people think pornography is dangerous for other reasons.

Some feminists point out that a lot of porn depicts men behaving badly toward women: calling them whores and bitches, slapping and hitting them, making them have sex in awkward positions, penetrating them in ways that look painful. All this turns women into objects, say the feminists. It degrades them. Boys and men who watch porn come away thinking that cruelty in real-life sexual relationships is acceptable. They may even get the urge to commit crimes against women: everything from beatings to rape.

Many feminists also say that porn is so degrading that no woman would ever perform in it unless she had terrible problems, such as poverty, drug addiction or psychological trauma from being abused as a child. This means that porn consumers are supporting an industry based on women's suffering.

Another argument, often made by those in the mental health professions, is that pornography is addictive, like alcohol and heroin. According to this thinking, people (usually men) can start off enjoying porn, but then lose control, eventually spending so much time with it that they lose their friends and loved ones. They have to go to therapy to break the habit, or even to psychiatric hospitals.

Others interested in mental health think porn can be harmful to minors because they are not emotionally developed enough to understand the meaning of the sex they are seeing. According to this thinking, sexual images can shock children, and this shock can become fixated in their minds for years.

Meanness, violence, addiction, shock: it all makes porn sound frightening and dangerous. Warnings issue from church pulpits, school health classes and the news. But many people look at porn anyway. Many feel guilty and worried.

What is hardly ever discussed are the facts about pornography and its effects on people. Instead, most of the people we hear from are spouting opinions based on their religious or political beliefs rather than on scientific and scholarly research. Scientists, who are mainly psychology, sociology and communications researchers at universities, look for objective ways to understand pornography. They design studies. They talk to porn viewers and porn makers, asking them about how porn makes them feel and act, and often administering psychological tests. Using the information produced by these studies, researchers have found no convincing evidence that porn is harmful to adults or children.

But these findings rarely make it to the wider culture, and the researchers' work almost never gets discussed. Their findings are drowned out by gloom-and-doom talk and calls for more Internet filtering, more therapy sessions for porn "addicts," more laws to keep minors away from sexual images and words.

As a result, very few people know that porn has not been shown to cause mental illness or crime. Even fewer have heard arguments from religious leaders, feminists and mental health professionals that porn is beneficial for many people. It can help adults who grew up ashamed of their bodies and sex. It can provide a substitute for people who feel sexually aroused but don't have sex partners. Think of prisoners, travelers and singles who are separated from husbands, wives, boyfriends or girlfriends. They can use porn to masturbate or otherwise feel sexually satisfied. This "virtual" approach can be safer — and often kinder, gentler and cheaper — than hitting the streets in search of a casual hook-up.

And, there is the undeniable fact that many people simply enjoy porn and feel they have no problems with it at all.

On the other hand, much porn does show men acting cruelly and violently toward women. XXX-rated materials may not cause males to go out and attack the opposite sex, but considering the reality of real-world violence against women, it is depressing, even infuriating, to see the same behavior shown on videos and DVDs.

Another troubling feature of porn: the possibility that users will confuse fantasy with reality, and end up hurting the feelings of people they care about.

Consider how porn actresses look and act, even when the sex they're engaging in seems relatively consensual and enjoyable rather than cruel. For the most part, their breasts are big and hard because they've been enlarged through surgery. Their bellies are flat from long workouts at the gym. Their genitals are waxed, making them look more like those of girls than grown women. On tape, these actresses are always ready to jump into bed, and when they do, their bodies are perfectly smooth and rhythmic. Their moves are astoundingly acrobatic — "like circus art," as one porn director describes them, "like an athletic performance." They engage in all kinds of sexual acts, from anal sex to having partners ejaculate on their faces. They are almost never shown using birth control or safe-sex aids such as condoms.

In the real world, how many people's bodies, behavior and sexual preferences are like these? Very few. But porn performers' looks and moves aren't supposed to be like most people's. Like those perfectly made-up and clothed models in fashion magazines, they are the stuff of fantasies.

For people who use porn — especially for teens and twentysomethings who are still on a steep learning curve about sex — the challenge is to understand that what they are seeing and hearing is performance, not real life. Without that understanding, hardcore porn can cause confusion and problems. A male who has gotten most of his sex education from porn may think that his girlfriend is supposed to look and act just like a starlet. He may pressure her to do things she doesn't want to do. This can damage a relationship, even end it.

But for those who have learned enough about the world to separate fact from fiction, porn is no scarier or riskier than anything else on television, film, DVD or the Internet. Starting from infancy, children watch thousands of hours of mainstream media, and much of what they see and hear is tasteless and violent. There is much more violence on TV and in Hollywood movies and video games than there is in porn. By the time they enter adolescence and adulthood, young people have already seen countless staged assaults and murders. Some critics call these performances trash and complain that they coarsen our culture. Others claim that seeing violence in the media makes people act violently in the real world. But there is no evidence for this cause-effect relationship, according to many researchers who have tested this claim with studies. Their findings and arguments constantly get aired in the mainstream media — because after all, it's the mainstream media that's being attacked by the criticisms. People who research porn, on the other hand, almost never get a hearing on prime-time TV or in family newspapers.

This book does not sing porn's praises or recommend that people use it. But it does not condemn porn, either, as something that is especially dangerous and evil. The purpose of this book is to give readers information so they can decide for themselves how to deal with the world of "adult entertainment" in modern media and culture. Some will already have seen a good deal of porn. Others, little or none. Some will have found it fun and exciting, and others will have felt bored, disgusted or deeply troubled. Still other people will have had different feelings at different times. Each experience is common. Because everyone has a unique background and personality, there is no one way to feel about porn.

This book looks at the facts about porn: its history, how it is made and distributed, the way it is talked about in our culture, and the data scientists have gathered as they try to measure its effects on people. It aims to help readers understand and deal with pornography — not just in our personal lives, but as citizens, too. Local and national governments have a lot to say about this issue, some of it intelligent and reasonable, but much of it confused and fear-driven. Misinformation and panic make for policies that hurt society rather than help, and that is as true for laws about porn as for other regulations. Learning the facts is thus a first step to understanding, and then entering the public fray when porn is discussed. There is a lot of finger pointing in that fray, a lot of screaming and excess emotion. It can seem confusing and overwhelming. How, then, to lower the volume and clarify the conversation? The information you'll find in the following chapters will help.

Chapter 2
A Brief History of Porn

Where, exactly, did pornography come from? Has it always existed or is it something recent? Most importantly, what is pornography?

According to the dictionary, the word pornography comes from the Greek *porne*, which means prostitute, and *graphos*, meaning writing. Using these roots, pornography means "writing about prostitutes."

But that is too simple. A good deal of writing about prostitutes would never be called pornography — articles and books by social workers, for example, who specialize in helping sex workers. On the other hand, a lot of writing that seems pornographic does not mention prostitutes at all. In addition, porn does not have to be written. It comes in the form of photos, videotapes and DVDs, computer graphics, cable TV programs and telephone chat lines.

Other definitions of pornography sound technical but do a better job of describing it. In *The Invention of Pornography: Obscenity and the Origins of Modernity*, Lynn Hunt defines porn as "the written or visual presentation in realistic form of any genital or sexual behavior with a deliberate violation of existing and widely accepted moral and social taboos," and the "explicit depiction of sexual organs and sexual practices with the aim of arousing sexual feelings."[1]

In plain language, for something to be pornography, it has to give clear details of people behaving in a sexual manner, especially by emphasizing their genitals (for women in our culture, this includes breasts). Second, it must concentrate on these sexual parts and activities for one main reason: to get people sexually aroused. Third, and most important, pornography should seem "dirty." Users are supposed to feel that the people who made it knew they were doing something immoral, and that by reading, looking at or listening to porn, consumers are also behaving badly. Pornography is shameful, a secret pleasure to be roped off from the rest of our lives.

Using this definition, it turns out that most of what we think of as porn today has been around for less than 400 years. It was almost unknown until the seventeenth century. But what about Greece and Rome, those ancient civilizations often called the cradles of today's Western culture? Visitors to art museums with exhibits of statues, carvings, dishes and paintings from these ancient regions cannot help noticing that many show naked people and sometimes people having sex. When Pompeii, the Roman city that was buried by a volcanic eruption in AD 79, was dug up in the 1700s, many murals and frescoes were discovered of people having sex. These wall decorations were found in rooms used not just by adults but by youngsters as well. Even childrens' bowls had sex scenes painted on them.

Rome also produced a lot of sexual writing. Very few high-school students take Latin classes anymore, but those who do may have studied works by poets like Catullus. In a poem quite typical for him, Catullus tells a woman named Ipsitilla that he is coming to her house and that she should have "ready for me nine consecutive copulations" because he has an erection that shows through his tunic.

Sexy stuff, and it probably caused people thousands of years ago to get aroused. Still, it was not pornography to the ancient Greeks and Romans, because they did not think it was immoral. Their cultures celebrated nudity, and the depiction of sexual activity on household and art objects was perfectly acceptable. The work of Catullus and other poets shows that writing and reading about sex was not disapproved of, either.

What began to change all this was the rise of Christianity. The early Church had a far more negative view of sex than the Greeks and Romans did. According to the New Testament, the person who worked hardest to make the young religion popular was Saint Paul. He preached that sex between husbands and wives is necessary to make children, but sex with anyone else, for any other purpose, is strictly evil. In a Bible passage that sums up Paul's views, he warns the Romans that "to be carnally minded" — to be interested in sex for sex's sake — "is death."

Despite this negative attitude toward sex, many sexually explicit images were created during the Middle Ages. The Pierpont Morgan Library in New York City, for instance, has a collection of exquisite, hand-written prayer books from the 1200s. They contain gilded illustrations of religious themes — as well as illustrations in the margins of tiny, naked, copulating people. Churches built during the same period in France are decorated with sculptures of buttocks, men's genitalia and naked women. Art historians doubt that the conscious purpose of these sculptures was to arouse viewers. Instead, the sexual images were always coupled with gargoyles and devils. Sex was associated with hell as a warning to people not to commit sins. Even so, it is not hard to imagine churchgoers getting very mixed messages.

By the Renaissance in the 1500s, artists were creating paintings with explicitly sexual themes. Florentine artist Agnolo Bronzino painted *Venus, Cupid, Folly, and Time* in the 1540s. This painting shows the Roman deities Venus and her son Cupid, both nude, with Cupid fondling his mother's breast and kissing her lips. *The Martyrdom of St. Agatha* by Sebastiano del Piombo, depicts men tearing at a woman's breasts with pliers, preparing to hack them off with a knife. Today it would qualify as hardcore sadomasochism. During the Renaissance, it was painted to hang in a church. Michelangelo also created erotic material. He unveiled *The Last Judgment* in 1541, a fresco that showed hundreds of naked bodies, including graphic genitalia. It was commissioned for the walls of the Vatican's Sistine Chapel.

The subjects of this Renaissance eroticism were saints and Greek and Roman gods and goddesses, not ordinary people. That would change with the advent of the metal printing press, invented by Johannes Gutenberg in 1450. The first book he produced was a Bible, but within a few decades, the presses were rolling with sexual scenes involving everyday humans. In 1524, the Italian poet and satirist Pietro Aretino, designer Giulio Romano and engraver Marcantonio Raimondi published *I Modi*, later translated into English as *The Sixteen Pleasures* or *The Postures*. The book originally contained sixteen engravings of men and women in different sexual positions. Each was later accompanied by a lewd poem by Aretino ("Open your thighs so that I can clearly see your beautiful ass, with your cunt in view," went a typical verse). Over the next two centuries *I Modi* was translated and printed throughout Europe.

A more instantaneous success was Francois Rabelais' *Gargantua and Pantagruel*, written in France between 1530 and 1540. It tells the story of two giants, Gargantua and his son Pantagruel, and their travels with Friar John and the scholar Panurge. The book uses sex and humor about excrement to spoof war, law and religion. In one scene a woman scares the devil away by exposing her vagina. In another, Panurge scatters musk on a fine lady who has rejected him, which excites all the dogs of Paris into mating. Rabelais boasted that *Gargantua and Pantagruel* sold more copies in two months "than there will be of the Bible in nine years."

The authorities were not fond of such books. When Pope Clement VII found out about *I Modi*, he ordered all copies burned, jailed engraver Raimondi, and made re-publication punishable by death. But counterfeit versions followed over the next few decades, as the number of sonnets increased to twenty and the number of sexual postures almost doubled from sixteen to thirty-one. *I Modi*, *Gargantua and Pantagruel* and other sexually oriented literature became so abundant that the Church issued the Index Librorum Prohibitorum, a list of everything Catholics should not read. *I Modi* was one of the first books to be included in the index.

Books with sexual themes were not the only ones on the black list. The Church also worried about writings by scientists such as Galileo and religious literature inspired by its new rival, Protestant Christianity. Protestants believed that people should read and interpret the Bible by themselves, without the intervention of priests. They also insisted that Christians did not need Popes to make religious law or take parishioners' money. These heretical ideas naturally disturbed Catholic Church officials. Often, they were more concerned with books promoting Protestantism and anti-clericalism than with books that dealt with sex.

But the Popes had a difficult time separating sex writing from anti-Church writing, because many books combined both topics and used sexual material to attract attention to their criticisms of ruling institutions. Seventeenth- and eighteenth-century European intellectuals were developing the philosophies of materialism, which denied the existence of the supernatural, and humanism, which considered the human race rather than God the highest form of existence, and libertinism, which celebrated the senses, all of which are involved in sexual pleasure. Writers who promoted these philosophies attacked the Catholic Church and its anti-sexual attitudes. That is why a good deal of libertine writing, including the work of the Marquis de Sade, depicts sexual acts set in churches and monasteries.

By the time of the French Revolution in the late 1700s, it was common to criticize and ridicule kings, queens and other nobles by writing about them having sex, or by making engravings of them in outrageously sexual positions. One widely circulated pamphlet depicted Queen Marie-Antoinette in the midst of an orgy. During this period, the French government banned many books. Some were about sex; some were strictly political. Jean Jacques Rousseau's *Emile* mixed the two themes and was banned for what the government called "bizarre and dangerous opinions." Despite these restrictions, sexually themed writing flourished.

By the 1800s, however, most of the politics had disappeared from sexually themed writings. In 1789 the French had seen how sexual writing and imagery could encourage people to turn against their rulers. Now, after the revolution, the new authorities did not want a repeat performance, and they cracked down on political literature that used sex as a theme. Meanwhile the middle class was expanding in much of Europe. Members had more leisure time, more income, and a greater desire to be entertained, including by sexually explicit but not necessarily political materials. The novel was becoming a very popular form of literature, particularly among women. Men, too, were enjoying novels, including those with frankly sexual themes that could be used as an aid to masturbation.

Fanny Hill, or the Memoirs of a Woman of Pleasure, published in England in 1749, is an early example of this genre. Its heroine, Fanny, is a prostitute. Many of her adventures show how the rich exploit lower-class people, and in this sense, *Fanny Hill* is a political piece of writing. But Fanny's sexual exploits have always been the biggest draw. By 1820, the book was a bestseller in Europe and was being smuggled into the US. Soon home-grown American sex novels were being written and sold quietly. Meanwhile, American women wanted information about how to avoid getting pregnant, which involved talking about sex. Several pamphlets and books were published about birth control.

Until the 1600s, the well-educated upper classes were practically the only people who could afford sexual art and writings. By the 1800s, these materials had become inexpensive enough that even the working class could buy them. This frightened authorities, particularly in countries that were becoming industrialized, and where tensions were increasing between the poor and the rich. In nineteenth-century England in particular, the upper classes feared that workers would stop working hard if they were exposed to sexually charged materials. During Queen Victoria's long reign, England, continental Europe and America became terrified of masturbation. Before this time, people who disapproved of masturbation quoted from the Bible and its warnings not to spill one's "seed" without the possibility of making a baby. Now, doctors began making "scientific" claims that masturbation made young people ill and drove them insane. By the end of the 1800s, boys caught masturbating often had their penises put into painful contraptions to keep them from touching themselves again. Girls had parts of their genitals burned off.

Given these extremes, it should not be surprising that sexual books and pictures were thought to be very dangerous — for children, poor people and women. Educated, upper-class gentlemen could, perhaps, look at these sexual materials without harm. But everyone else must be kept safe. As if to mark this fear, England passed a law in 1857 forbidding the sale and distribution of sexual materials considered "obscene." During the same year, the word "pornography" first appeared in the Oxford English Dictionary. Now, the only people allowed to see sexual materials were a few male judges, male art collectors and male police agents. Meanwhile, an entire, society-wide conversation developed around trying to figure out what was allowed and what wasn't, who could look and who couldn't, and what awful things might happen if the law was not enforced.

And thus, pornography was born. In documentary film

producer Fenton Bailey's 1990s television series, *Pornography: The Secret History of Civilization*, he concludes that the attempt to define pornography "is a trick question, since essentially no such thing exists. It is only naming the thing that creates it." The naming of pornography separated representations of sex from everyday life. Naming crystallized those representations into a taboo that everyone discussed and obsessed over. And the more pornography was discussed and obsessed over, the more of it there was.

The nineteenth-century explosion in porn was also the result of a new technology: photography, which was invented in 1827. Some of the first photographs ever made were of naked people and people having sex, and by the 1860s, it was very easy to buy postcards showing these scenes. When cinema was developed in the late 1800s, some of the first moving pictures also showed people having sex. The earliest surviving American film showing intercourse is known today by the title *A Grass Sandwich*. It is said to have been shot in New Jersey in 1915. By the World War I era, there were many other films like *A Grass Sandwich*. They were called "stag movies," and could be seen at men-only parties. In Hollywood, meanwhile, some directors included scenes with actresses appearing nude from the waist up, but only until the 1930s.

Beginning in the Great Depression era, mainstream films were forbidden from showing frank portrayals of sexuality. The bedrooms of married couples even had to be furnished with twin beds. Within a couple of decades, though, so-called "art" theaters — often located near universities — were showing foreign films that were much franker about sex. *And God Created Woman* starred the French actress Brigitte

Bardot and debuted in the United States in 1958. The film featured sensuous views of Bardot's posterior and steamy shots of her baring her amply endowed chest. It blew the lid off of sexuality in the non-pornographic cinema.

By the 1920s and 1930s, there was a growing market for pornographic magazines in the US. Cheaply produced comic books nicknamed "Tijuana Bibles" often made fun of movie stars by publishing cartoons of them having graphic sex. "Nudist" publications such as *Sunshine and Health* supposedly promoted the fitness benefits of not wearing clothes while doing everyday activities such as playing volleyball. Their main appeal, though, was probably that readers could stare at photographs of naked people. Nudist magazines could not show genitals or pubic hair, however, and readers who wanted to see this level of nudity had to buy "art photography" magazines.

"Men's magazines" became very popular during and after World War II. They followed on the heels of a huge market among soldiers for sexy "pin-up" photos of Hollywood stars. Men's magazines ran pictures of naked or barely clothed young women, with their pubic hair covered or airbrushed. Like all pornography, these publications were considered to be for the lower class. This changed in 1953, when a young man named Hugh Hefner launched the new men's magazine, *Playboy*. Its nude models were carefully chosen for their all-American, middle-class, suburban girl-next-door looks. *Playboy* also published articles about music, travel and politics, and it was the first porn magazine that was considered urbane and sophisticated instead of perverse and sleazy. *Playboy* was soon selling hundreds of thousands of copies a month. Several similar magazines followed in the 1960s and tried to compete by showing their models' pubic hair. But none had as many readers as *Playboy* did.

On the heels of *Playboy* came the porn movie industry. Early films lasted only a few minutes and repeated over and over in "loops." The films were installed in machines that a customer activated by inserting quarters. Each quarter would buy a couple of minutes of viewing time. The machines and movies were called "peep shows" and they were located in private booths in porn bookstores. Customers would watch the films and masturbate. By the early 1970s, however, the US was dotted with hundreds of little buildings belonging to the Pussycat Theater chain. These theaters showed porn films and were often located near porn bookstores. Again, the audience was almost all men who often masturbated while watching the movies in the dark. The theaters were unsanitary, located in seedy parts of town, and had bad reputations.

Even so, many movies proved very popular. One was *I Am Curious Yellow*, a politically themed film from Sweden that featured completely nude characters, including a young woman caressing and kissing a man's genitals. Another was *The Immoral Mr. Teas*, directed by Russ Meyer, whose photography had appeared in *Playboy*. *Mr. Teas* was part comedy and part cheesecake. It focused on women with large breasts in different stages of undress, but did not include sex.

Films such as these may even have influenced the mainstream film industry, since Hollywood was releasing films with explicit sex scenes by the late 1960s. These films included the award-winning *Midnight Cowboy*, with Dustin Hoffman, and *Last Tango in Paris*, starring Marlon Brando. In turn, Hollywood also influenced porn. Hardcore sex movies of the 1970s featured many performers, such as Harry Reems and Georgina Spelvin, who had been trained as actors. Directors often wrote scripts that included long, involved plots and dialogue. *The Devil in Miss Jones*, starring Spelvin and released in 1973, dealt seriously with suicide and sexual repression. *Deep Throat*, a comedy about fellatio starring Linda Lovelace, cost about $25,000[2] to make and earned back over $50 million. Men flocked to porn theaters to see it. And for the first time, so did women.

The porn movie industry died when videotape was invented. Sony introduced the videocassette recorder in 1975, and within thirteen years most North Americans owned one. Porn movies were among the first to be transferred to video, and the market for porn on video got the VCR and videotape industry up and running. Entrepreneurs soon stopped using film and instead recorded porn directly onto videotape. Unlike film, porn videos could be produced in just a few hours. There was little effort made to create interesting stories or dialogue, because that would have taken too much time and performers would have had to rehearse.

Still, the industry boomed. Porn became more popular after the first AIDS cases surfaced in 1981 and the world gradually became aware that masturbation and other sexual activities involving fantasy were far safer than sex with a partner who might be infected with HIV. In addition, the California State Supreme Court made it legal to shoot adult films because performers were now considered to be actors instead of prostitutes. Before this change in regulations, video shoots were held in secret and were sometimes raided by police. Today, thousands of porn videos are produced every year in the US, Japan and Europe. They can be rented at video stores and viewed on cable television by subscription or in hotels on pay-per-view channels.

Today the video business is being overshadowed by newer technology: the Internet. The World Wide Web was developed in 1994, and the first graphical browser came into use a year later. As was the case with the printing press, photography, movies and videos, porn was one of the first products featured on the web and it jump-started the online market. By 1998, it has been estimated, Internet porn was bringing in $1 billion in revenue — between 5 percent and 10 percent of all the money made online. Porn on the web includes everything from still pictures to streaming video and live web-cam performances. Porn chat rooms are also available, where people use the keyboard to carry on sexually oriented conversations.

Meanwhile, back in the lower-tech world, sexual conversation is available over the telephone for a fee. Strip clubs are thriving. Mainstream bookstores sell "erotica" — another name for porn that is considered "softer," or less explicit, than XXX-rated material. Print, photography, television, audio, bytes and bodies: all are mixed up together in today's adult entertainment industry, creating a wallpaper behind everyone's lives — including young people's.

Despite — or maybe because of — this ever-present background of sexual imagery, the endless, anxious discussion of earlier times continues today. Will porn unleash chaos and drive society to the dogs? Will it hurt the kids? Is it bad for women? Who gets to look? Who decides? Perhaps these questions are what keeps porn going, even expanding. Maybe they are porn's real definition.

Chapter 3
Pornucopias of Fantasy

Sixty-year-old "Jay" (not his real name) is one of many American men who regularly use pornography. Over the years, he has seen technology change how porn is made and consumed. When Jay was a teenager in the early 1960s, he started looking at men's magazines like *Playboy* when he visited a neighbor — a grown man — who collected them. By the time he was a young man, he was buying the magazines at convenience stores and bookstores. In the 1970s, he often went to theaters that screened XXX-rated movies. On his way home from work he visited strip clubs, where women dance nude. The mostly male audiences who patronize these clubs pay the women who work there to sit and drink with them and do individual performances, called "lap dances." Jay also used to rent videotapes and DVDs to watch at home. When out of town on business trips, he watched pay-for-view movies in his hotel room. And during the last few years, Jay has learned a bit about computers. He knows how to download sexual images from the Internet to his hard drive. But he's not savvy enough to keep up with the flabbergasting range of new porn technologies.

When porn first appeared on the Internet, it was in the

form of writing and still photography. Later, chat rooms developed where people could have real-time sexual conversations. Since the late 1990s, many other forms of Internet pornography have become common. Today there is streaming video, which makes it possible to watch and download the same kinds of adult-entertainment material that earlier was shown only in movie theaters or on television screens. Now, thanks to the web cam, a computer user can watch live sex performed by people who might be thousands of miles away. Viewers can even send messages to web-cam performers, telling them which sexual acts to do next.

It usually costs money to be admitted to commercial websites that use these new technologies. But many sites offer free samples to recruit new subscribers. In addition, "amateur" sites are very popular on the web. People who are not necessarily trying to make money from porn can post still images and streaming video on these sites. They trade digital porn with each other, using methods like "shareware."

Exactly what is on all these websites? No one really knows. Studies done since 2001 have found that between 1.5 and 2.4 percent of all web pages have pornography on them — that's one out of every 41 to 66 web pages. But the studies give few details about the content of these sites.[1]

One way to get an idea of what is available is to examine some of the most popular commercial material. BushDVD.com is a large Internet rental company that adults can join by paying monthly dues. Members order up to eight porn DVDs at a time, receive them by mail, send them back after viewing them, then order more. The company keeps 23,000 different productions in stock. Its website classifies each one according to dozens of categories.

One big category is called "Gonzo." In this genre the sex is wall to wall, without any effort to tell a story, and performers act as though they're being filmed, often by looking into the camera and directly addressing the viewer. Another genre is "Pro-Am," where one or two performers are industry professionals, but the others are (supposedly) amateurs. A common theme in Pro-am involves a man walking up to women on the street and asking if they want to have sex with him. If they agree, he takes them to a hotel room or apartment to be filmed. "Amateur" deals with people who depict themselves as spontaneous, one-time performers more interested in exhibitionism than money. In "Girls Gone Wild" videos, young women at street parties (at New Orleans Mardi Gras, for example) are invited to flash their breasts for the camera in exchange for a cap, beads or other cheap souvenirs. Another important category is labeled "Feature." DVDs in this class have a storyline and often show a white, heterosexual couple having sex that's nicknamed "Vanilla." That means it is sex that is commonly practiced and generally considered acceptable. The "All Girl" category, which includes many DVDs, features women having sex with each other.

"Young" is also a very popular genre. To perform legally in porn, actresses must be at least eighteen. Those chosen for the "Young," or "Barely Legal," genre are not much older, and they often dress in schoolgirl clothing for their performances, with their hair in pigtails. "Interracial" mostly presents black men having sex with white women. A white woman pornography producer interviewed for this book said that her biggest orders for "interracial" porn come from white men living in the US South. That region, of course, is where black people used to be held in slavery, and where laws separating blacks and whites lasted until just a few decades ago.

Many genres also involve intense aggression, but not always sexual aggression, against both men and women. In a series featuring women dressed as Catholic nuns, the actresses scold men by calling them names and whipping them with belts and paddles until their legs and buttocks are covered with real welts. Another style, "bukake," focuses on groups of men who take turns ejaculating on crying women. And many films show distraught women being tied up, with clamps and clothespins applied to their breasts and genitals.

It might seem unpleasant, even horribly repulsive, to think of this kind of porn. Many people might question why white men would seek out images of black men involved with white women. Why would viewers — who are overwhelmingly grown men — enjoy watching teenaged girls having sex? Who wants to beat men and torture women? No doubt about it, porn comes in so many varieties that everyone who sees a good deal of it is bound to be offended by something. In order to understand why there is so much variety, and why so many aspects of pornography seem especially offensive, we need to understand fantasies.

Here is how the *Encarta World English Dictionary* defines fantasy: "An image or dream created by the imagination. The creation of exaggerated mental images in response to an ungratified need. An unrealistic or impractical idea."

Several words in this definition of fantasy explain what is going on in pornography. "Imagination" is the first important term. Something from the imagination does not have to exist in reality. Dreams are an example of this. They are often very detailed and can pack a strong emotional punch. But they tend to make little sense compared with the real world. Dreams about floating or flying through the air or about being a baby again, for example. Or nightmarish scenarios about falling from a tall building or being in a high-speed car crash — then walking away uninjured. These things can't really happen. Yet they are powerful products of the imagination.

As we see from dreams, it's easy to imagine things that are, as the definition puts it, "unrealistic or impractical." But even if they would never occur in the day-to-day world, imagining them can be comforting and pleasurable. That is especially so when the imagination works to answer "an ungratified need." Think, for example, of people who were forced into concentration camps during World War II and given almost nothing to eat. As prisoners got hungrier and hungrier, many started to imagine huge, gourmet meals. They knew they couldn't possibly have food like this while in the camps, but they fantasized about it anyway. Likewise, people whose loved ones have died may spend a lot of time fantasizing that the deaths never happened and that their family life hasn't changed — even though they're well aware that it's not true. And people who have been wronged by others often develop detailed revenge fantasies, complete with scenes of terrible violence.

Children also spend a good deal of time fantasizing. They can get very involved, for instance, with superheroes and action figures with magic powers, such as being able to fly. Many psychologists believe that superhero characters are popular because they help small, helpless youngsters feel more powerful and safe. Maybe that is why very few parents forbid their children from playing with action figures. Instead, they explain that although Superman can fly, real people can't, so don't try jumping out of windows! Adults understand that children's fantasies can be harmless, even helpful, when handled appropriately. Pornography, too, is fantasy. It has almost no direct relationship with the real world, but it gives some people comfort and pleasure. And that is probably what makes it so popular.

It goes without saying that porn fantasies are about sex. It is so taboo in our culture to discuss or even think about sex, people who fantasize about it often enter what feels like strange and forbidden territory. Because pornography creates words, sounds and images to hang sexual fantasies on, it can also seem very strange. This is true even of "vanilla" sex. A man and woman in this type of porn may have oral sex and intercourse, but it happens completely differently from how it does in the real world. In one typical "feature" DVD, a young man who works at a store delivers groceries to a beautiful young woman who answers her door with her skirt pulled up. The two are strangers. They say almost nothing to each other. There's certainly no talk about needing birth control or a condom to prevent pregnancy or AIDS. The woman doesn't seem at all nervous. She leaps into wild sex with the man and both quickly have orgasms. They smile and go their separate ways.

Scenes like this are appealing fantasies for men for two reasons. First, they objectify sex — making it seem like a thing, rather than an emotion or a relationship between people. Psychotherapists Michael Thompson and Dan Kindlon point out that boys learn early on how to think of sexual pleasure as a kind of object. In their book *Raising Cain: Protecting the Emotional Life of Boys*, they write that "by adolescence a boy wakes up most mornings with an erection. This can happen whether he is in a good or bad mood, whether it is a school day or a weekend… Boys enjoy their own physical gadgetry. But the feeling isn't always, 'Look what I can do!' The feeling is often, 'Look what *it* can do!' — again, a reflection of the way a boy views his instrument of sexuality as just that: an object." The penis is an object before women are objects, write Thompson and Kindlon. It "makes its own demands."[2] Porn extends the habit of objectifying women and sex.

Second, porn also makes getting sex from women seem effortless. In the real world, boys have traditionally been raised to think of themselves as always wanting sex and having a right to it. At the same time, girls are taught that women aren't nearly as amorous as men, and that if they want sex too much, they are sluts.

This mismatch creates unhappy situations when it plays out in bed. It's made worse by the strains of everyday life: hard days at school or work, money problems, headaches, worries about pregnancy and disease, worries about "what people will think if they find out I did this." If real-world sex were a meal, the chicken would rarely be hot enough and there would not be quite enough dessert to go around.

Porn, on the other hand, is often "all about the fantasy of abundance," says California sex therapist Marty Klein.[3] It's like a fairy-tale feast where the food is perfectly prepared and there's more than enough for everyone. Even better, the diners didn't have to buy or cook it — it was no work or trouble at all. And the variety of dishes is amazing. Many, such as roast beef, new potatoes and chocolate cake, are enjoyed by almost everyone. Others — the Brussels sprouts, duck pâté and pickled watermelon rinds — make just a few people's mouths water, while others absolutely can't stand them. Regardless of their likes and dislikes, the guests line up at the buffet to load what they want on their plates. No one wonders about what childhood experience made them like funny little green vegetables more than potatoes. No one thinks that watermelon rinds are evil. They just pass them up for the cake. Everyone gorges. Afterward, heartburn is never a problem.

Likewise, porn shows endless examples of trouble-free sexual expression, even when the imagery is grotesquely violent. Many boys and men feel insecure and angry about the fact that real-world women often refuse male sexual advances. Porn scenes that show women being humiliated and assaulted may be revenge fantasies. Still, it is only pretend. In the real world, it is a serious crime to rape or otherwise attack someone. But in the XXX world, the victim is an actor, the DVD ends, and the viewer walks away happy. Someone else might be bored, disgusted or frightened by the same production. Ultimately it's very hard to say why different people (including women) have such different fantasies — and therefore such different tastes in porn.

It will probably always be impossible to say for sure why erotic images vary so much. Suffice to say that each person is an individual, with different life experiences. Sexual fantasies speak to those experiences, and so does porn. Most people who use XXX-rated materials understand that they're about imagination, not reality. Just as people who like horror and action movies almost never go out and commit murders, porn viewers generally know that sexual fantasies — even strange, dark, violent ones — are fictions that can be enjoyed in private and don't have to be put into practice in the real world.

With that in mind, it is easier to understand, for instance, why an older man might enjoy porn that features eighteen-year-old actresses. Maybe the most exciting sexual experience of his life was with his first girlfriend when he, too, was a teenager. Perhaps watching porn helps him remember that time and the happiness he felt then. He probably has no interest in actually having sex now with an eighteen-year-old, but simply rents DVDs from the "Young" category to indulge a harmless fantasy.

According to Joseph Slade, who has studied pornography for over three decades, porn also makes users feel as though they are breaking taboos.[4] That feeling is probably what explains Southern US white men's taste for porn that shows black men having sex with white women. Until a few generations ago, this kind of sex was so forbidden in the South that blacks who got caught engaging in it (or who were even accused of it) were often killed — hanged, then set afire by white men. People in interracial relationships still face hostility and discrimination in the US, especially in the South. Porn showing black men with white women breaks the taboo. That is what makes it a pleasurable, powerful fantasy — for some people, at least. For many others, it's a sign of white racism, or just a turn-off.

Anyone who explores the wide range of porn is bound to find themes they enjoy and themes they find offensive. The trick is to understand that all of them are fantasy, and even when fantasies seem repulsive, the vast majority of people who have them go through the real world acting like ordinary, decent human beings — grandfathers, fathers, brothers and yes, grandmothers, mothers and sisters. The expression of our fantasies in porn can sometimes make our attractions to pornography seem weird and deeply disturbing. But dreams can also be strange and troubling — yet we are usually glad that we are able to dream.

Amateur Porn

One of the most popular styles of porn these days is made by ordinary people with little or no interest in being paid for their performances. The Internet teems with websites devoted to photos and videos of men and women who look as though they just got home from the laundromat or grocery store — then took off their clothes and had sex.

Known as "amateur" porn, it is made by husbands and boyfriends who take pictures or videos of their wives and girlfriends. The wives and girlfriends may also do the filming. If a person is solo, he or she often aims the camera at him or herself. The results are then posted on the Internet — generally for free, though video makers may get a few dollars for their effort.

The range of body types in amateur porn is astounding. There are conventionally good-looking, youngish people with flat stomachs and buffed muscles. But plenty of others are overweight, saggy and old enough to be grandparents. The only thing these people have in common is that they want the world to see them in pornographic poses.

Long-time pornography researcher and Ohio University scholar Joseph Slade has a theory about why amateur porn is so appealing. He says that "modern culture is largely consumer-oriented and hostile to humanism"— the concept that the world should revolve around individuals, not the "invisible hand" of buying and selling.[5] Much of the porn industry is dedicated to making profits. But at the same time, porn represents an effort to reach out for intimacy and transparency — for nakedness. And amateur porn does that better than any other genre.

Chapter 4
Who Uses Porn?

Go shopping in just about any big food store in the US or Canada and you are likely to find racks of paperback books near the checkout counter. "Romance novels," they're called. They sell hundreds of thousands of copies each week, and their reading audience is almost all women — ordinary women who buy their family's groceries. Romance novels never carry XXX-rated warnings. Anyone can buy them, even minors. But look inside and it is clear that they can be as steamy as porn.

Take *Between Strangers*, by Linda Conrad, which came out in late 2004 and was published by Silhouette Books. The heroine falls for a good-looking man, and after they have known each other for a couple of days they have sex. "When he covered a breast and flicked a thumb over the hardened nipple, she cried out, thrusting against his hand," one passage begins. "Then she pressed a palm against the hardened length straining behind his fly." The scene continues with the couple engaging in explicitly described intercourse, complete with adjectives like "throbbing" and "wet," and the verbs "writhed," "moaned" and "plunged."[1]

A similar genre exists for teen girls, including the recent

novel *Rainbow Party* by Paul Ruditis. In this novel, a group of girls goes to a party, each wearing a different colored lipstick. When all the girls have performed oral sex on the boy partygoers, each boy will have a "rainbow" on his penis. This book was reviewed in mainstream publications and sold in major bookstore chains.

For years, women and adolescent girls have been reading titillating romance novels, even as conventional wisdom claimed that pornography was just for men and that its purpose was to help them masturbate (as early as the seventeenth century, English writer Samuel Pepys was writing in his diary about "books that you read with one hand"). A few generations later, men were buying "French postcards" from vendors on city streets — pictures of naked people and people having sex. Women and children almost never purchased them. Men in the early twentieth century had parties where they screened sexually explicit movies. These parties, and the films themselves, were often called stags — after the old word meaning male animal. Women never came to these affairs unless they were prostitutes.

Pornographic magazines and movies became more available after World War II. But their main audience was still almost all men. They were often referred to as "the raincoat crowd," after the idea that anyone who used porn was a poor, uneducated pervert who might walk around naked under a raincoat and pull the coat aside to shock people. That idea was reinforced by the fact that porn movie theaters were usually located in seedy parts of town that respectable people avoided.

But in the early 1970s, a handful of blockbuster porn films, including *Deep Throat*, attracted some women to porn theaters, although they almost always went with their boyfriends or husbands. And in the 1980s, when videotapes replaced film in porn distribution, audiences didn't have to go to theaters anymore to see dirty pictures. Now they could rent them at neighborhood stores and watch them at home. Soon it was common for middle-class housewives to visit video outlets and rent three different videos. One would be a Disney movie for the children's afternoon viewing. The second was a mainstream Hollywood production for the whole family to watch after dinner. The third was a porn tape, which the woman and her husband would watch late that night. By the late 1980s, almost half of porn videotape renters were women.

The Internet has since created an even bigger audience for porn that includes men, women and even children. It's supposedly illegal for minors aged eighteen and under to have access to online porn. They see it anyway — sometimes by accident, sometimes on purpose. Statistics show that the notion that male porn users are poor and uneducated has also fallen by the wayside. A survey done in 2000 found that most visitors to the fifteen most popular adult websites had incomes of at least $50,000 a year.[2] As the figures in this chapter's "Porn Census" reveal, these trends seem to be getting even stronger as time goes by.

Porn Census

Number of adult-entertainment websites in 2000: 60,000.
Number of adult-entertainment websites in 2004: 1.6 million.[3]

1 percent of all websites in 2000 were "adult" in nature.[4]
40 percent of all Internet traffic in 2000 was to this 1 percent of "adult" websites.[5]

34 percent of Internet users visited adult websites in 2005.[6]
50 percent of guests at hotel chains, such as Holiday Inn and Marriott, order pay-per-view porn.[7]

In 2001, 25 percent of regular North American visitors to adult websites were women.
In early 2007, 48 percent of US visitors to adult websites were women.[8]

Young Porn Users

About six in ten nine- to nineteen-year-olds in the UK who go online at least once a week have seen porn there (mostly by accident).[9]
One in four eight- to eleven-year-olds in the UK say they deliberately visit online porn sites "sometimes" or "often."[10]

45 percent of US teens aged twelve to seventeen say they have one or more friends who regularly view and download Internet porn.[11]

35 percent of eighth-grade boys in Alberta, Canada, say they have viewed Internet porn "too many times to count." 8 percent of eighth-grade girls say the same. Most of the boys and almost half of the girls who've seen porn say they logged on deliberately.[12]

Average age when California high school boys first see porn: eleven.
Average age when California high school girls first see porn: twelve.
41 percent of Californian high school boys and girls thought their run-ins with online porn were "no big deal."[13]

Chapter 5
Does Porn Cause Rape?

Ted Bundy was an American serial killer who confessed to raping and murdering thirty young women in Washington, Utah, Colorado and Florida between 1974 and 1979. Murder is punishable by the death penalty in many US states, and Bundy was sentenced to be executed. The night before he was put to death in 1989, he was interviewed on TV by Dr. James Dobson, head of the moral-conservative Christian organization Focus on the Family. Bundy told Dobson he was addicted to violent pornography, and he looked at it before he committed his murders. Until this eleventh-hour interview, Bundy had never connected his crimes to pornography, and no porn had been found at his home when it was searched. Even so, people who argue that porn causes sex crimes often make their point by mentioning the monstrous Ted Bundy.

It is not surprising that they do. Bundy is an ugly but dramatic poster child for the idea that pornography is dangerous — even though research has never proved this claim. As sex therapist and researcher Dr. Judith Becker has pointed out, sex crimes committed by adults and teens are linked to childhood sexual and physical abuse and to being drunk, but not to being exposed to pornography. According to a recent study by University of Toronto researchers, pornography plays a role in the crimes of very few sex offenders.[1] Findings such as these go back to the 1970s, and society used to agree with them for the most part. Back then, pornography was becoming easier to get in the US than ever before, and authorities wondered if it caused adults and young people to commit crimes. The US Commission on Obscenity and Pornography was established in 1968, under the politically liberal administration of President Lyndon Johnson, to try to answer this question.

In 1970, after several months of hearing testimony and reviewing research, the commission found no evidence that exposure to or use of sexually explicit material hurts society or individuals. In fact, the commission added, porn was probably keeping would-be sex offenders from misbehaving by helping them vent aggression that might otherwise make them assault people.[2]

Investigations in other countries over the next several years reached similar conclusions. The British Home Office "Report on the Committee on Obscenity and Film Censorship," released in 1979, noted that "We unhesitatingly reject the suggestion that the available statistical information for England and Wales lends any support at all to the argument that pornography acts as a stimulus to the commission of sexual violence." A 1984 report by the Canadian Department of Justice also found no connection.[3]

Porn, harmless? Conservative politicians and anti-pornography feminists could not believe it, especially because XXX-rated materials seemed to be getting more violent in the 1970s. So more studies were done in the

1980s. A group of psychology researchers, including Edward Donnerstein, Neil Malamuth and Dolf Zillmann, tried to see if violent porn made people — men, especially — feel more aggressive toward women, or develop negative attitudes toward them.

The researchers had a tradition to borrow from. Several psychologists during the 1960s and 1970s had done similar investigations on children to see if watching violent television programs would make them act aggressively. In one famous experiment, some nursery school children saw a film of the cartoon character Herman the Cat in which he behaved non-aggressively. Another group saw a film of a real adult hitting a large Bobo Doll. The kids from both groups were then treated in ways that made them feel frustrated. After that, they were given a chance to hit Bobo Dolls. Children who had seen the adult hitting the doll hit their Bobos in larger numbers than the kids who had watched gentle Herman the Cat.[4]

Even so, a 1972 report by the office of the US Surgeon General, "Television and Growing Up," was cautious about this study and others. The study did not prove that TV violence caused real world violence, it only suggested it, said the report. A cause-effect relationship could be shown only in children who already tended to be aggressive. Overall, the report warned, the effect of TV was "small compared with many other possible causes, such as parental attitudes or knowledge of and experience with the real violence of our society." What went on in a child's own family and neighborhood was considered far more important than what he or she saw on television.

The TV-and-kids studies got a lot of press, but the US

government has never moved to outlaw depictions of violence on television (or in Hollywood, either) — even if the violence shown is against women. But in the late 1970s and the 1980s, as feminists and conservatives rallied against porn, new research was designed that piggy-backed off the old Bobo Doll work.

One now famous study, published in 1981, signed up eighty male college students as volunteers.[5] Some watched a film that showed a woman being raped and looking as though she was enjoying it. Another group saw a rape that obviously upset the victim. A third group saw a young couple having consensual sex and looking happy. And a fourth saw a film with no sex or violence at all.

Afterward, the students met with a man or woman from the research team. Some of these team members acted mean and insulting to some students, but pleasant to others. Then the students were all told they could give an electric shock to the research team member they had just talked with. (The shock machine was fake, but the researchers kept that a secret.) Students who had watched rape films before meeting with a mean female researcher gave the most shock. Even students who had been treated nicely tended to give stronger shocks to female team members if they had seen a rape film. This experiment, the researchers concluded, provided evidence that violent porn can make men feel more aggressive toward women.

In a study done by Neil Malamuth and J. Check, male and female college students listened to one of several short stories about sex.[6] In some stories, a woman was raped and became aroused by the attack. In others, a woman was raped and seemed very upset. Other stories described a woman willingly having sex; in some, she seemed aroused, and in others, disgusted. The researchers found that both male and female students got more sexually aroused by stories in which the woman got aroused than they did when she seemed upset — even if she was being raped. In another study, male students heard a story about a woman who is raped and gets aroused. When questioned later, more study volunteers who heard that story thought that women enjoy being raped than did volunteers who had not heard it. From these studies, the authors concluded that media depictions of women being raped and enjoying it could encourage people — men, especially — to believe that women in the real world like being raped. That attitude could encourage men to commit rape.

Studies like these have been widely publicized since 1986, when the US Department of Justice held hearings for the Attorney General's Commission on Pornography. Better known as the Meese Commission, it was organized during the politically and culturally conservative Republican administration of President Ronald Reagan. Critics noted that the Meese Commission was stacked from the beginning with witnesses who did not like porn and felt it should be banned.

The Meese Commission also ignored research that found *no* negative effects from porn. Instead, the commission played up research, like the 1981 "electric shock" study, to claim that porn causes violence and negative attitudes toward women. The commission's bias even disturbed scientists whose work suggested that porn might make people behave badly in the real world. One was Neil Malamuth. He had done the studies in which men were read short stories about rape.

"There is currently no research to show long-term effects [from pornography] on aggressive behavior," wrote Malamuth and two other colleagues in a statement later distributed by the American Psychological Association. They went on to mention a study some of them had done that discussed the lack of evidence for "long-term effects." Even so, the psychologists complained, "The main body of the 1986 commission's report... did not include any reference to or discussion of this study." The Meese Commission's generalizations "may be premature," they added.[7]

Malamuth and his co-authors also pointed out that according to most studies, violence is the primary factor in porn that causes bad behavior in the lab, not sex. One writer, Daniel Linz, did research in which men spent five days watching either non-violent porn or R-rated slasher films, which show extreme violence toward women but are considered fairly mainstream. The subjects who saw slasher films were more desensitized to violence against women than the porn watchers were. But even if violence was the culprit and not porn, Linz and his fellow researchers warned against rushing to ban slasher films — or anything else, for that matter. As scientists, they favored looking for alternatives to censorship.

Despite all this discussion, controversy and uncertainty, the claim that porn causes violence and bad attitudes has been pushed so much by the news media that today it almost seems like fact. But it isn't. The only real fact is that after dozens of studies, scientists still don't know if porn makes men more likely to hurt women or think poorly of them. They may never know, because taken as a whole, the research is full of problems.

Is There a Relationship between Sex Crime and Porn?

In the mid-1960s, when the availability of porn in the US was just beginning to explode, a group of investigators allied with the famous sex researcher Alfred Kinsey reported their finding that in general, people who committed sex crimes had seen less porn than other people.[8] And sex offenders were hardly swinging liberals. Usually, they were deeply religious, and socially and politically conservative.

Subsequent research has come up with similar findings. Studies show that sex offenders tend to have had sexually repressive upbringings and that their parents taught them very conservative attitudes toward sex.[9] A 1973 study found that as teens and adults, sex offenders tend not to have used porn any more than other men — and often they've used less.[10] One investigation looked at sixty teenaged boys who had committed sex crimes and examined four factors that might come into play when youths commit sexual offenses: pornography, substance abuse, and being sexually or physically abused. The boys in the study who drank alcohol had more victims than those who did not. Sexually or physically abused boys had more victims than those who had not been abused. But most of the teens said porn played no role in their crimes.[11]

For one thing, many studies have had different results than the ones that have gotten wide attention. Many have found no difference in people's tendency to act aggressively, approve of rape or insult women, regardless of whether or not the research subjects have looked at porn — even violent porn. Why don't we hear about these studies? Because to be published in a scientific journal, a study usually has to find a difference between people who have been exposed to something (like porn) and those who were not exposed. No difference, no publication. Which means the mass media never hear about the research, so the public doesn't, either.

And even in studies that do link porn to negative behaviors, it is very hard to tell if there is a connection between what people do when they are serving as research guinea pigs and how they act in real life. Almost all the research has taken place on just a few US university campuses, with mostly white, middle-class students as volunteers. It's a narrow population. The volunteers know they're in a lab, not the day-to-day world where cultural norms and the law discourage men from committing sex crimes or saying bad things about women.

Meanwhile, in the real world, researchers have performed studies of entire nations that challenge the idea that porn leads to sex crimes. In fact, these studies suggest just the opposite. Researchers have been very interested in Denmark, for example. In the 1960s, this country went through a "porn wave." But instead of banning or censoring pornography, in 1969 the government lifted all restrictions on porn for people over sixteen. Sex crimes went down instead of up. In later decades, when West Germany and Sweden also liberalized their pornography laws, these countries' rape rates also decreased or stayed about the same.[12]

Japan is another fascinating case. An extraordinary amount of porn has become available there since the 1970s, and much of it shows extreme violence and kinkiness — everything from people having sex with animals and dead bodies, to depictions of brutal sexual assault against women. Yet Japan has one of the lowest rape rates in the world, and from the 1970s to the 1990s, that rate also went down as the availability of porn shot up.[13]

Experts have tried to guess why sex crime is rare in Japan and why it has decreased even more during the last generation. Some believe that Japanese culture traditionally puts great emphasis on restraint, and this keeps people from acting out what they see in pornography. Others point out that most sex offenders begin their assaultive behavior in childhood, and over the past three decades, Japanese children have been spending more time with stay-at-home mothers and other adults who are trying to tutor them so they can get into good schools and colleges. "We believe this in itself reduces the opportunity for anti-social or criminal activity and helps socialize the child to avoid criminal behaviors as an adult," write Diamond and Uchiyama.[14] They also think new sex education programs in schools are partly responsible for declining rates of sexual violence in Japan.

In light of all these studies and observations, it is wrong to conclude that pornography causes sex crimes or anti-social ideas toward women. This is something researchers agree on, not just in the US, but also in Canada, Europe and Asia.[15] But they also agree that porn is not problem-free.

Chapter 6
The Feminists' Arguments

> Pornography is the theory, and rape the practice.
> — Feminist writer Robin Morgan[1]

> If we're going to talk about oppressive images of women, we'd better include laundry soap commercials.
> — Feminist writer Lisa Palac[2]

> If feminists define pornography per se as the enemy, the result will be to make a lot of women ashamed of their sexual feelings... And the last thing women need is more sexual shame, guilt, and hypocrisy — this time served up as feminism.
> — Feminist writer Ellen Willis[3]

Criticisms of pornography that are based on the teachings of fundamentalist religion are easy for non-fundamentalists to ignore. The idea that God frowns on sex outside of marriage, sex for entertainment or sex for any reason other than for making babies — none of it packs a punch among people who don't believe that every sentence in the Bible or Qur'an or Torah is true. The claim that pornography causes rape and other crimes is a far more powerful argument against porn for many people, because it comes from psychologists, not churches. Still, as we have seen by exploring this claim, it doesn't stand up to scientific review.

But there is a third anti-porn argument. It has been promoted by some feminists who think that pornography, in and of itself, does terrible damage to women. This argument isn't religious. It isn't scientific. It's political, and because many people sympathize with the political movement for women's rights, it is probably the most compelling of the anti-porn arguments. Some men who avoid using porn say they do so because they sympathize with feminism. Likewise, some men who use porn say feminism makes them feel guilty about it. Governments and courts in the United States and Canada have used feminist theory to ban pornography. Conservative politicians — who are usually opposed to women's rights such as legalized abortion — regularly use feminist arguments to try to outlaw porn.

But feminist anti-porn arguments are controversial even among feminists themselves. The women's movement is far from united on this issue, and has been divided for years. If we go back in time to the beginning of the rift, we can get a better idea of why many feminists want to ban porn — and why many others think this is a bad idea.

Modern feminism took root in the UK, Canada and the United States during World War II. With the country's young men overseas fighting fascism, there weren't enough bodies to fill all the jobs back home. So millions of women started punching time clocks, doing all kinds of work, including dirty factory labor that had always been thought of as strictly for men. The new employees did fine. They felt powerful and independent. Their governments and the media showered them with praise for helping their nations.

Then the war ended and the men came back from overseas. Women were urged to stop working, marry, have babies and be housewives. Most did all these things, but as the 1950s wore on, a large number became frustrated. Their daughters felt the same way. By the early 1960s, many of this younger generation of women were involved in the efforts to gain civil rights for African Americans and other racial and ethnic minorities, and the movement to end the war in Vietnam. The time was ripe for a movement for women's rights. By the late 1960s it had started growing. Soon it was going full tilt.

Newspaper classified sections during this period still advertised jobs for men only and women only. Women's work — as secretaries, waitresses and the like — paid less than men's, and feminists worked to desegregate jobs and make salaries identical for both sexes. That effort focused on economics. But feminists also looked at women's personal relationships with sexuality and men. They wanted to understand how a society ruled by males — a patriarchy — makes it seem normal and natural for women to be treated as second-class people in both private and public life. They wanted to attack patriarchal relations from the bottom up. That included challenging negative images of women in books, magazines, advertisements, movies, television and even album covers. Feminists were especially disturbed by images that showed women enjoying being beaten or raped. And they were angered when women were portrayed as "objects" — skimpily dressed, naked, doing housework while wearing high heels, or otherwise acting as though their main purpose in life was to make men happy.

Acting on these concerns, feminists in 1968 chanted and performed street theater in Atlantic City, New Jersey, to protest the Miss America Pageant, the annual beauty contest featuring women in low-cut evening gowns and revealing bathing suits. In the 1970s, American feminist activists demonstrated against Hugh Hefner's Playboy Clubs — whose all-woman wait staff dressed in tiny costumes with bunny-rabbit tails and ears. When *Snuff,* a movie featuring the fictional sex murder of a woman, opened in New York City's Times Square in 1976, hundreds of people walked a picket line outside the theater for several evenings. New groups such as Women Against Violence in Pornography and Media were formed on the East and West coasts. One organization protested against a billboard advertising a Rolling Stones album, which showed a bruised, tied-up woman saying "I'm 'Black and Blue' from the Rolling Stones — and I love it!" The billboard was removed. Protests expanded to areas of cities where porn movie theaters and bookstores were concentrated.

Early feminists did more than just challenge the idea that women are objects for men's pleasure. They also tried to figure out what pleasure meant for women *themselves.* Traditional Western culture, particularly since the late eighteenth century, has viewed females as not being interested in sex, which is supposed to be a male concern. Now, the feminist movement urged women to learn what turned them on: to get familiar with their genitals, masturbate, explore their fantasies and tell partners what they wanted during sex.

By the end of the 1970s, though, feminism was under

fire from a conservative backlash — a push from the political right to roll back the clock on the last decade's civil rights gains. Abortion had been legalized in the UK in 1967, in Canada in 1969, and in the United States in 1973. But now, a right-wing movement was growing to outlaw it again. Conservatives noisily blamed feminism for "killing unborn babies" and, because women were leaving home and going to work, for "destroying families." By the early 1980s, feminists felt under fire.

It was getting harder for women's rights advocates to talk about the patriarchal roots of economic inequality. They were criticized for denouncing media images of women in traditional occupational roles such as stay-at-home mom. They were called prudish and ugly when they took on fashion magazines, which they said promote the message to millions of women that they should be skinny and wear certain clothes, makeup and hairstyles. Most of all, feminists found it more difficult to promote women's sexual liberation — or anyone else's. The sudden appearance of AIDS in the early 1980s put a huge damper on that discussion.

One topic became easier for feminists to criticize, though: pornography. Like many other forms of media, much porn is sexist. It is mostly created and used by men. It concentrates on male fantasy, which often includes indifference to and cruelty to women. In many ways, porn's view of the world is not so different from what is shown on TV and in Hollywood. It's just a lower-rent version that puts sex front and center. But that makes porn easier to criticize than mainstream media. In addition, as feminist writer Judith Levine has pointed out, rape and sexual assault are real dangers for women in the day-to-day world. So it's understand-

Porn or Erotica?

Gloria Steinem and many other anti-porn feminists make a distinction between pornography — which they disapprove of — and "erotica," which they feel is acceptable, and even positive for women. So-called "erotica" is said to put sex within a larger context. An "erotic" movie may have an involved plot and prominent mainstream actors. Erotic literature also embeds sex in a bigger story and may use a sophisticated writing style. Many feminists say that erotica portrays sex between equals, whereas in porn, one person is oppressing the other.

Writing in 1978, Steinem claimed that erotica is "a mutually pleasurable, sexual expression between people who have enough power to be there by positive choice," while "pornography is about dominance."[4] Feminist writer Diana Russell associates porn with "abuse" and "degradation," whereas erotica is "free of sexism, racism, and homophobia, and respectful of all human beings."[5]

Critics say that erotica is simply pornography with better production values, made for better educated, richer people who need to rationalize their enjoyment of sexy materials with the pretense that it is "art." Thus, the same people who are often horrified by the raunch on the populist Internet are mostly untroubled by elite institutions such as the Louvre, in Paris — where young and old alike can stare at Rubens' *Marie's Education*, the seventeenth-century painting with a naked woman fondling her genital area, as though she is masturbating. Feminist film critic B. Ruby Rich agrees that social status and personal taste lurk beneath the argument. "[W]hat is pornography and what is eroticism?" she asks. "One is bad, the other is good (guess which). Fixing the dividing line is rather like redlining a neighborhood: the "bad" neighborhood is always the place where someone else lives. Porn is the same. If I like it, it's erotic; if you like it, it's pornographic."[6]

able that they would be tempted to focus on pornographic images as stand-ins for their fears about sexual violence.[7] Conservatives, of course, had their own reasons for despising porn. But now feminists joined their attacks.

A powerful critique came from Canada, in the form of a

documentary. *Not a Love Story*, made by filmmaker Bonnie Klein, looked at the making of hardcore porn movies. Klein interviewed young women whose work in XXX-rated films gave them sexually transmitted diseases and otherwise harmed them. Internationally famous feminists such as Robin Morgan and Kate Millett appeared in the documentary to second Klein's contention that pornography damages performers and that it encourages male viewers to objectify women.

Meanwhile in the US, radical feminist Andrea Dworkin and law professor Catharine MacKinnon were leading the feminist anti-porn effort. Dworkin was a former prostitute and political radical who had been sexually assaulted by police officers after being arrested in the late 1960s for protesting the war in Vietnam. Dworkin believed that in patriarchal societies, all sex between men and women is a violent assault against women, no matter how pleasant it seems. "Romance," Dworkin wrote in one of her books, "is rape embellished with meaningful looks." Describing dating, she added that "In seduction, the rapist often bothers to buy a bottle of wine."[8]

If all sex between men and women is rape, it follows that pornography is just another nasty part of the assault. Dworkin and MacKinnon promoted the idea that porn is more than just words and pictures that might give some men bad ideas about women and lead them to violence. They said that porn by its very nature is hurtful. It always reinforces men's ideas that women are inferior and deserve to be raped. This makes it a violation of women's civil rights. As MacKinnon put it, "Pornography is what it does, not what it says."[9]

The Snuff Film Myth

In the 1999 movie *8MM*, Nicolas Cage plays a detective hired by lawyers for the wife of a recently deceased elderly tycoon. She had opened his safety deposit box and found something very disturbing. It appeared to be a "snuff film" — it shows the brutal murder of a young actress who thinks she is working on a run-of-the-mill porn or slasher production, but who seems to be deliberately murdered as the cameras roll. When the lawyer asks whether snuff films really exist, Cage says he thinks they are "kind of an urban myth."[10] Of course, he soon finds out otherwise. After all, *8MM* is Hollywood fare.

In the real world, Cage would have been right the first time. Snuff films do seem to be urban myths — as fictional as the tale of the woman who put her freshly bathed poodle in the microwave to dry it, and accidentally baked the poor pup. Stories like that are not true, but they're widely thought to be, and they never die. The same goes for rumors about snuff films.

The myth began in the 1970s, when film producer Allan Shackleton bought distribution rights to a low-budget slasher movie titled *Slaughter*. It had bombed after playing in just a few theaters, and Shackleton made plans to add a faked sex murder. Meanwhile, he changed the title to *Snuff* and began claiming it had footage of a real homicide. Before he had even added the new material, the media was describing the film as though it had genuine murder scenes.

Snuff opened in January 1976 in a New York City theater. It was picket-

Dworkin and MacKinnon claimed they were different from religious fundamentalists and conservatives. As feminists, they said, they weren't against porn simply because it involves sex. In the early 1980s the two tried to get the city council of Minneapolis, Minnesota, to pass an anti-pornography law. The law stated that if a violent crime were committed against someone and police found that the attacker had used pornography beforehand, the people or company who produced the porn could be sued for violating the crime victim's civil rights. Because porn producers could never know in advance if their products might fall into the

ed by outraged feminist protestors. The furor only added to the movie's popularity. Soon the New York City Police Department was warning that other snuff films existed.[11]

Outrage about snuff movies launched "Take Back the Night" anti-porn marches in North American cities, from San Diego to Toronto. Many activists believe that these demonstrations launched the feminist anti-porn movement. As anti-porn leader Laura Lederer wrote, "*Snuff* was the powder keg that moved women seriously to confront the issue of pornography."[12] Ironically, *Snuff* was originally co-produced and co-directed by a woman.

Many phony snuff films have since been made. In addition, many real crimes have been captured on video and film, then made available for public viewing. The John F. Kennedy assassination film is one example. The beheading of *Wall Street Journal* reporter Daniel Pearl by Islamic fundamentalists in Afghanistan is another. A few sex killers have also filmed their victims during the homicides.

But as far as authorities know, no murder has ever been committed so that a recording of it can be distributed for profit. There are people who will do virtually anything if the money is right, no matter how brutal. But cinematic and digital special effects make it very easy these days to stage pretend killings that look completely believable. So it may not be worth the legal risk to produce a real snuff film when it is so easy — and convincing — to make a fake one.

hands of people who would later commit crimes, the Dworkin-MacKinnon law would have strongly discouraged the production of porn.

The Minneapolis City Council passed the law, but the mayor vetoed it. He said it was unconstitutional because it violated the right to free speech. Dworkin's and MacKinnon's ideas got attention from other officials, however. But often these people seemed less interested in civil rights for women than they were in the old reasons for banning porn — that it shows people having sex in order to arouse viewers. In 1992, for example, the Canadian

Supreme Court issued the Butler decision, calling porn "degrading" and "dehumanizing" to women, and deciding to keep in place Canada's old obscenity laws, which make it a crime to produce a work whose "dominant characteristic…is the undue exploitation of sex, or of sex and any one or more of the following subjects, namely, crime, horror, cruelty and violence." The Canadian Supreme Court admitted that there is no evidence showing a direct connection between porn and discrimination or violence against women. Even so, the judges said, mere "belief" in the connection was reason enough to outlaw pornography.

Using the Butler decision as justification, Canadian customs officers have stopped plenty of porn at the border. Ironically, much of this supposedly obscene material is en route to gay men — who by definition aren't interested in having sex with women — and to lesbians, who don't orient to sex with males. Some lesbian and gay porn focuses on sadomasochism (S&M), which shows people being tied up and whipped. In gay male-oriented porn, the person taking the assault is a man, not a woman. In lesbian bondage porn, the person with the whips and nasty words is a woman. It is hard to imagine how this homosexual material could be thought of as anti-woman. This has not prevented it from being stopped at the border. Canadian customs inspectors have especially targeted gay and lesbian bookstores. Their shipments from abroad, even books by world-famous authors such as Jean Genet, have often been seized. A Vancouver bookstore, Little Sisters, sued the government over this problem in the 1980s, and the Supreme Court ruled in 2000 that customs cannot discriminate against gays and lesbians when enforcing the obscenity law. The "feminist" Butler decision, however, remains in place. And ironically, it keeps Canadians from reading books by Andrea Dworkin, one of the law's main inspirations.

Dworkin is the author of political novels criticizing rape and sexual aggression toward women. One, *Ice and Fire*, has passages like this: "We are on the beach. Mister wants some sex… He is wired, tense, has spasms, shows me his knife… He fucks me." Because of the "cruelty and violence" in passages like this, *Ice and Fire* and other Dworkin books are banned in Canada.

Dworkin's and MacKinnon's ideas about pornography have been accepted by many women's rights advocates. But they've been strongly rejected by many others. As writer Susie Bright commented shortly after Dworkin's death in 2005:

> Every single woman who pioneered the sexual revolution, every erotic-feminist-bad-girl-and-proud-of-it-stiletto-shitkicker, was once a fan of Andrea Dworkin. Until 1984, we all were. She was the one who got us looking at porn with a critical eye, she made you feel like you could just stomp into the adult bookstore and seize everything for inspection and a bonfire.
>
> The funny thing that happened on the way to the X-Rated Sex Palace was that some of us came to different conclusions than Ms. Dworkin. We saw the sexism of the porn business…but we also saw some intriguing possibilities and amazing maverick spirit. We said, "What if we made something that reflected our politics and values, but was just as sexually bold?"[13]

While Susie Bright imagines what women-oriented porn would look like, other feminists defend the male-centered material that already exists, even though they don't particularly like it. Journalist and essayist Ellen Willis, who died in 2006, believed that the slogan "pornography is violence against women" is just code for the traditional claim that "men want sex and women endure it." And though a lot of porn *does* show men acting badly toward women, much of it presents the opposite: women tying men up, then abusing them verbally and physically.

Furthermore, feminist scholar Lisa Duggan notes that porn degrades women no worse than do "non-sexual images of gross violence," or "advertising images of housewives as dingbats obsessed with getting men's shirt collars clean."[14] The real problem isn't porn, anti-censorship feminists argue — or even fashion and laundry soap ads. Instead, it's the economic and cultural institutions that keep women as second-class citizens and lead to those insulting images. Change the institutions that encourage sexism, these feminists say, but keep government out of the business of regulating images.

Many feminists are against all censorship, including that of pornography. One of the main reasons for banning porn during the past two centuries has been to "protect" women's supposedly innocent, delicate minds. But the group Feminists for Free Expression (FFE) strongly criticizes this reasoning. The non-profit organization was formed in 1992 to oppose book, movie and music banning. FFE believes that censoring in order to attack problems such as violence against women is "cosmetic" as well as "dangerous." "Censorship traditionally has been used to silence women and stifle feminist social change," says FFE on its website.

"There is no feminist code about which words and images are dangerous or sexist. Genuine feminism encourages individuals to choose for themselves."[15]

And increasingly, women *are* choosing for themselves, even when the choice is to view porn — or make it. As they do, it is becoming clear that pornographic images mean different things to different people, both men and women. An image that deeply offends one woman can be fun and sexy to another. This shouldn't surprise. Writer and pornography fan Lisa Palac explains that women have "rich sexual fantasies, powerful libidos and the power to choose" what to look at and read.[16] Feminist activist Ann Snitow agrees. Because pornography "glorifies male supremacy and sexual alienation, it is deeply reactionary." On the other hand, sometimes it "includes elements of play, as if the fear women had toward men had evaporated and women were relaxed and willing, at last." That fantasy, Snitow writes, can be "wishful, eager and utopian," for women as well as men.[17]

Pornography is full of contradictions. But so is the women's movement. And the feminist argument against porn is far from the last word on the subject.

Chapter 7
The Business

Wander far into the huge hall at Las Vegas' Venetian Hotel, and you could almost forget where you are. The crowds are thin at the back, and the walls are lined with tiny kiosks. At one of them, four smiling, ordinary-looking women old enough to be grandmothers are hawking piñatas. Traditionally, piñatas are filled with candy and hung from the ceiling at parties in Mexico. When they are knocked down, the sweets spill out. At their little stand in Las Vegas, the American women boast that they assembled their piñatas themselves. A dealer at another booth beckons you to touch her custom-made dolls. With her sensible jacket and big glasses, she could be a weekend vendor at an arts-and-crafts show.

But this is no housewives' convention. It's the 2005 Adult Entertainment Expo, a days-long extravaganza that markets pornography to dealers from all over the world. The piñatas are in the shape of naked men and women, complete with outsized penises and breasts, and they sell for about $100 each. The dolls cost $6,000 apiece. They are the size of an adult and are fabricated from a special material that makes them look and feel just like live, nude women.

The salon-styled hair on their heads is real, and all their body orifices open, from the mouth down. The doll dealer hopes to get a few dozen orders for her product. The piñata makers would be happy with a few hundred.

Meanwhile, at the mobbed entrance of the Expo hall, much bigger business is on display. Exhibits for giant adult entertainment firms like Vivid, VCA and Wicked Pictures spread over thousands of square feet. The walls are plastered with billboards of nipples, derrieres and feet in spike heels. Television screens wink non-stop with hardcore scenes. And — the showiest draw of all — glittery porn starlets slink around, posing in the flesh and little else. Male fans who have paid a forty-dollar entrance fee line up to caress and squeeze these women while their friends snap souvenir photos.

In a few hours, the starlets will appear in evening gowns at a flashy awards ceremony. It will look like Hollywood's Oscar fest, except that here, a typical prize category will be "Best Group Sex Scene." After the awards are handed out, industry bigwigs will go to parties. They will drink, chat and make deals. Some will be big deals, because porn is big business.

Before VCRs made it possible for people to rent videotapes for home viewing, porn was a small, sleepy part of the US economy, pulling in at most $10 million a year in the early 1970s.[1] It was even less important in other countries' economies. But today, consumers worldwide can watch porn on cable and satellite TV in their homes. They can order it as "pay-per-view" at hotels. They can visit Internet websites. They can call 800 and 900 numbers for phone sex. They can buy sex toys by mail order, at stores, and even at house parties. They can visit "gentlemen's clubs" to see strip shows by young women (and sometimes young men). They can purchase magazines such as *Maxim* and *Playboy* from convenience stores.

They can also view videos and DVDs. In 2004, there were over 800 million rentals of porn productions from stores nationwide in the US. "And I don't think it's 800 guys renting a million tapes each," says Paul Fishbein.[2] He is founder and president of *Adult Video News* (*AVN*), the porn industry's trade magazine. Each issue of *AVN* is over 350 pages long, including advertisements and video and DVD reviews. The people who write the reviews are kept very busy. By 2000, 11,000 adult titles were being produced each year. (Most were made in the northern suburbs of Los Angeles.) Compare that number to Hollywood, which released only 400 films during the same year.

The technical quality of those thousands of porn DVDs and videotapes runs from excellent to terrible. Some are made in hi-tech studios by expert directors and camera operators. Many others look as though they were shot in home basements by amateurs who barely read their equipment's instruction manual. No matter. Everything can be put on the Internet. And some of it will bring in money, because by late 2003, there were over a million websites serving up more than 260 million pages of erotic material. Of those, 70,000 were sites that charged customers money to look around.

Potential profit is large compared to many other industries. It is not unusual for an adult film that cost only $50,000 to make to bring in $250,000 — five times the original investment. And that's for a high-end production.

Many films cost only $15,000 to make, but they also bring hefty returns. Filming is often done in rented homes. Shooting lasts only two or three days. Videotape is used instead of much more expensive film stock. The actors and actresses are not union members. They get one-time payments for their work: usually $1,500 a day for white women working in the US, and just a few hundred dollars for men.

After the films are finished they are easy to sell. Hardcore versions can end up in rental stores. They can also be edited to make softcore versions (with no penises or penetration visible.) Softcore pornography can be shown on satellite, cable or hotel pay-per-view TV. Still shots from the films can be posted on the Internet and clips can be featured on streaming-video websites. Lately, producers are making deals to put images on cellular phone screens. Even sounds are saleable. Porn megastar Jenna Jameson's voice began emanating from cell phones in 2005 as "moan tones."

Thirty years ago, porn was available only in seedy movie theaters and out-of-the-way magazine stores. Back then, those who made and sold it seemed as sleazy as their merchandise. Practically all were men. Few were educated. Many had Mafia connections. Today porn is out in the open, and many of the producers are a different breed.

A few, like website operator Danni Ashe, are women. She used to be a stripper and nude model, but in the early 1990s she discovered the Internet and taught herself how to create a website. Today it is called Danni's Hard Drive, and it is one of the biggest adult entertainment sites on the Internet. In 2006, Ashe sold her company to Penthouse Media Group — publisher of the men's magazine *Penthouse*, for $3 million.

Candida Royalle was formerly an actress in porn movies; now she produces and directs them. Her company, Femme Productions, focuses on women viewers and their sexual pleasure. For Royalle, that means putting female performers on equal footing with males. It means setting sex scenes within a story or plot. It means fewer close-ups of female genitals. And, unlike in almost all male-oriented porn, Royalle's work avoids showing men ejaculating outside of women's bodies. Other women like Royalle who once performed in front of the cameras are also making their own porn — Veronica Hart and Nina Hartley, for example. All three women are now in their fifties.

Younger women, too, are directing and producing hardcore porn with what they consider to be a feminist sensibility. Some work at big studios that are trying to capture the growing female and "couples" porn-viewing market. Others, like Canadian director Angela Phong, are working at small companies such as Dirty Pillows in Toronto, which is run by women and produces lesbian-oriented "girl-girl" themed porn. This genre has been made traditionally for male viewers, using actresses who appear conventionally feminine — with long, styled hair, for example, lots of make-up and surgically augmented breasts. But lesbian-made and oriented porn often features actresses with natural bodies and unmade-up faces who look "butch" or masculine, often with bulky bodies and short haircuts. Lesbian porn is a very small part of the porn market because the big, male-audience-oriented studios are not interested. Lesbian material like Phong's is sold at feminist-identified sex shops, such as Good for Her in Toronto.

Younger women are also exploring aggressive and violent

themes in porn. A director who goes by the name Mason has made several videos in which actresses have very rough sex, which includes being dragged by the hair and ordered to bark like dogs. She says ideas like this come from her own sexual fantasies, and she considers her work to be woman-oriented. When she has been criticized as a woman hater, Mason has sometimes put on a burqa — an Islamic woman's full-body covering — to protest the veiling of female sexual expression.

Tristan Taormino, also a self-professed feminist, often includes scenes in her films that show women penetrating men with dildos. "I consciously work to create images that contradict (and hopefully challenge) other porn that represents women only as objects and vehicles for male pleasure," Taormino has written. "The lack of female pleasure in porn just sucks… I think making porn can be a political act, just as valid and valuable as other forms of activism within the women's movement."[3] Joanna Angel, co-founder of the punk-porn website BurningAngel.com, is a producer and performer. College educated and a self-proclaimed political activist, she was hired in 2006 by the US music magazine *Spin* to write a sex advice column. She often stars in hard-core productions that feature actresses in fishnet stockings, tattoos and Goth makeup. Angel, too, says she is a feminist.

So do the Suicide Girls. At suicidegirls.com, viewers — a large percentage of them women — can read music reviews and punk blogs, as well as post personal profiles and communicate with each other. They can also look at thousands of pictures of young, punk women in softcore poses that the models staged themselves. Like its models, most Suicide Girls employees — photographers, publicists and administrators — are women. They make what they call "alt-porn." Part of its appeal is that models have natural breasts and sport tattoos (and even eyeglasses). They also blog — often quite intelligently — about books and movies they like.

All this appeals to young men (and women) who identify with the youth counterculture. It gives socially conscious young men the feeling that looking at porn is not anti-woman. Even so, Burning Angel and Suicide Girls models look depressingly like those in mainstream porn. They may have big tattoos and torn clothes, but they are still over-whelming white and skinny. These conventions seem to reflect insider problems as well. In 2005, dozens of Suicide Girls models quit, complaining that they were being treated in sexist ways, including being called "whores." The focus of their anger was Sean Suhl, Suicide Girl's male co-owner and president. While the company has several women employ-ees, it is still typical of the industry in that it has a male pres-ident. Alt or not, porn remains a male-dominated industry.[4]

One of those dominant males is Bill Asher, but even he is a new breed. Asher is president of Vivid Entertainment Group. One of the world's biggest pornography producers, Vivid was turning out eighty porn DVDs a year by 2001. Asher graduated from elite Dartmouth College in New Hampshire, and he holds a master's degree in business administration. Vivid's feature productions use state-of-the-art technology. They each cost up to $100,000 to make. But executives like Asher are much more interested in the profits their productions can earn than they are in the flesh they show. Even Paul Fishbein, whose magazine *Adult Video News* reviews hundreds of adult films per issue, says the films don't interest him except "for business reasons." "My wife and I don't watch them for entertainment. It's hard for me to look at it as more than product."[5]

Some porn actresses are so business savvy that they have turned themselves into corporations. The most famous is Jenna Jameson. She became a star in the late 1990s after she signed a contract to make films with Wicked Pictures. Soon her films were making $15 million a year for Wicked, and she was earning hundreds of thousands of dollars a year for herself. Jameson then became chief executive of Clubjenna Inc., a porn website and movie production company. She co-wrote *How to Make Love Like a Porn Star*, which got significant media attention. She has appeared on the mainstream television series *Mr. Sterling*, in a major fashion campaign for Pony footwear, and in prestigious general interest magazines such as *Vanity Fair*.

One sign of the widening acceptance of porn is its profits, though estimates vary wildly depending on who provides the numbers. In 2000, *Adult Video News* magazine (*AVN*) claimed the industry had earned $10 billion that year in the US alone. *AVN*'s figure was repeated by most of the media and even by university researchers.[6] But in 2001, a reporter at the US financial magazine *Forbes* revealed that the $10 billion figure was not backed by reliable research and seemed greatly exaggerated. At most, he calculated, the adult entertainment industry netted about $4 billion in 2000, and even that estimate was generous.[7] In 2005, *AVN* claimed the industry made $12.6 billion that year — not much more than the $10 billion cited a half decade earlier.[8] In 2006 *AVN* said annual earnings remained at less than $13 billion.[9] These more recent figures could be accurate, or they could yet be too high.

But if they're correct — or even more or less correct — the porn industry is nothing to sneeze at. Thirteen billion dollars is more than the $9 billion Americans pay each year for theater tickets to Hollywood movies. It's half what the US gives other countries as non-military foreign aid. On the other hand, the adult entertainment business remains tiny compared to mainstream entertainment industries. In the US in 2001, for example, TV and radio earned advertising revenues of $54.4 billion. That's more than four times what the entire adult entertainment industry netted in profits, even according to the most generous estimates.

And adult entertainment includes more than just porn video sales and rentals. "Gentlemen's clubs," sex toys and hotel pay-per-view movies also enter the economic calculation. So does content made available on the Internet, but much — perhaps even most — of it is free, "teaser" samples or material posted by amateurs, people without much interest in making money. These freebies add little profit to the industry. But they do encourage people to consume porn. As one man interviewed for this book bragged, "I've been downloading it off the net for years and never spent a penny." Multiply his experience by millions of individuals, and it's easy to see how hardcore porn has so easily spread through our culture.

Hardcore porn also seems to have encouraged softer imagery in the entertainment mainstream: from regular displays of men's buttocks in the blockbuster HBO cable television series *Sex and the City*, to Janet Jackson's (probably planned) "wardrobe malfunction" during the half-time performance at 2004 Super Bowl Sunday, when one of her breasts was exposed. Softcore mainstreaming like this has probably helped open the XXX market to giant US companies that hardly anyone associates with porn. AT&T and General Motors subsidiary DirecTV, for instance, are part of the action, distributing hundreds of millions of dollars' worth of porn through their cable networks.

They keep this business quiet, though — AT&T's financial reports, for instance, do not break out profits from porn from profits earned, say, for cable-televised wrestling matches. Meanwhile, American companies such as Vivid, which openly publicize themselves as porn producers, have been reluctant to apply for listing on the US stock exchanges. They're nervous that Wall Street-related publicity could provoke controversy that would hurt their business.

Even so, some porn production and distribution companies had made it to the American Nasdaq by 2005. Private Media, listed on the stock exchange as PRVTMedia, is one. Based in Barcelona, Private is Europe's largest producer of pornography. The company makes one hundred features a year — about an eighth of all adult films made on the continent. Private then dubs its films into ten languages and sells them to vendors in forty-four countries. The Rhode Island-based company Metro Global Media (MGMA on the Nasdaq) is another company on the stock exchange. So are Playboy Enterprises (PLAA and PLA), New Frontier Media (NOOF) and On Command Corporation (ONCO), which distributes pay-per-view sex movies to hotels around the world.

The international market is also expanding. Porn films are being produced in France, Germany, Spain, the Netherlands and Hungary (which in 2005 made about 300 of the 1200 films turned out in Europe each year). In

Canada, hardcore programming for cable and satellite TV subscribers more than doubled during 2005. Other porn-related businesses are thriving: in Montreal, for example, agencies recruit good-looking young Canadians to travel to Los Angeles to act in porn productions. Hungary has a booming porn industry. So does Brazil. Japan produces more porn movies annually than even the United States, although Japanese products are not exported much because they are considered to be too poorly made and fetishistic for other countries' tastes.

Porn is no longer just about skin. Today it is also about dollars, Euros and practically every other currency in the world. Sex sells, goes the old saying. And today, sex seems ready to run the store.

Chapter 8
Workers

Christina Noir is not her real name. She uses the pseudonym so that fans won't find her in the phone book in Northern California, and so her family won't learn that she makes pornography. She says she enjoys having sex, mostly with men, while her husband, Matt, takes care of lighting and operates a video camera. Christina also likes the business of making porn: finding actors and actresses to be in her videos, locating places to film, and selling her products on the Internet after they're edited and packaged. She and Matt also have two websites where they recruit performers and sell tapes and other items featuring Christina. None of these enterprises brings in much money, so to pay the bills, Matt also works as a software developer. Christina, forty-two, homeschools the couple's grade-school-age daughter. When their little girl asks them what they do for a living, they tell her they "have a grownups' business."[1]

Matt and Christina represent a growing part of the pornography industry. Called the "amateur" sector, it's made up of performers who aren't having sex on camera to make lots of money. Instead, they like the idea of being photographed or videotaped and knowing their images will later be seen by strangers. Amateur photos pay little or nothing, while videos bring in $100 to $200 if they're sold to a big production company or a distributor. To earn more, performers must start their own businesses and pay out of their pockets for advertising. Often they don't bother. Or if they do, they keep things at the "mom and pop" level by putting in just a little time and money.

This part of the business is growing quickly. It's the part of pornography that critics have the most trouble dealing with. After all, it's clearly not about poor women being forced into sex in order to survive economically, because it hardly ever pays enough to live on. It doesn't seem to be solely or even mainly about women being pressured by abusive men, because women often share in the business side or manage it on their own. In short, a lot of pornography these days is being made by people — including women like Christina Noir — who seem happy with the work and don't find it particularly exploitive.

As we saw at the Adult Entertainment Expo in Las Vegas, the porn industry also has a "professional" sector, where the real money is made. This sector is controlled by a few big enterprises, including Vivid and Evil Angel, that each employ dozens of people and have their own studios and warehouses. They produce hundreds of porn videos and DVDs each year, and make millions of dollars in profit. At any given time, a few dozen superstar actors and actresses are working on contract for these big companies. These performers often make $100,000 a year or more. Their work is widely for sale on the Internet. They appear on home cable and hotel pay-for-view television. They go on tour, doing exotic dancing at "gentlemen's clubs" across the country.

Many have fan clubs. Some have started their own porn production businesses and, like Jenna Jameson, have even written books about their lives as porn celebrities.

These books — especially those written by women — often follow what seem like scripts. One story line describes porn work as fun, sexy and glamorous. Another, which is often quoted by anti-porn feminists, presents acting in porn films as a hell of abuse. Other memoirs tell a double-edged story. The actress starts out enjoying herself. Then she has serious problems. Finally, she leaves the porn business as an emotionally stronger, more independent person. *Lights, Camera, Sex*, by Christy Canyon, is a good example. It starts with Canyon as an eighteen-year-old who's been mistreated by her parents. She has dropped out of high school, left home, and tried to make it on her own as a clothing-store salesperson. But she can't earn enough money to get by. She goes into the pornography industry thinking it will only be about nude modeling, but gets tricked by her agent into having sex on camera. She vows to leave the industry, but she's quickly seduced by all the money she can make as a porn star. At first the sex is fun. After a few months, though, Canyon descends into drug addiction and depression. Eventually she kicks her drug habit and figures out how to make money in the entertainment industry without having hardcore sex. She writes a book about her experiences, which includes extremely graphic details about her porn performances.

Canyon's book and the others seem tailored to reinforce ideas about porn that people already have, or to titillate the same customers who watch the authors' videos and DVDs. The books have a fairy-tale quality — and at the same time, they're X-rated. It's hard to know what's true in them and what's hype.

A few books, such as Rachel Silver's *The Girl in Scarlet Heels: Women in the Sex Business Speak Out*, published in 1994, feature interviews with a number of sex workers. Most of the sex workers in Silver's book are British, and they have mixed feelings about their work. Some recall being exploited and victimized. Others say they enjoy what they do.

Tristan Taormino, the female porn director who considers herself a feminist, provides a good description of women who work in porn. "There are women who love sex and women who hate sex; women with low self-esteem and women with strong self-images; women addicted to plastic surgery and women with less than perfect bodies who like themselves just the way they are. I have met women who are sexually feisty, in control of their bodies, lives and careers; but there are also women who don't feel they have a lot of work options, who feel compelled to look a certain way to succeed, who are motivated more by money than anything else."[2]

Clearly, many industry insiders have stories to tell about workers and their reasons for being in porn. Meanwhile, sociologists with no axes to grind one way or the other have also looked at this group. In the 1990s, Sharon Abbott interviewed fifty actors and actresses working for the big production companies.

From her interviews, Abbott found that many porn workers were well educated. About a third of the people she talked with had graduated from college.[3] All of them had finished high school. Before working in porn, they'd held various types of jobs. Some — women and men — had been in the military. Many had been in retail sales. They left these jobs to take up careers in pornography for many reasons.

One was to make easy money. White actresses could

earn $500 to $1000 for shooting one porn scene, which would take only a half day. Men made much less per scene, but they often had more work over a year's time, and their careers lasted longer. Abbott found that women usually have to retire from acting in porn after two years, because they're no longer considered "fresh" and "new." Men's careers average five years.

On the other hand, working in porn costs a lot in personal expenses, especially for women. To look acceptable, they have to pay for pricey beauty treatments such as breast surgery and liposuction. In addition, women must buy elaborate clothing and costumes to wear at porn industry parties and for dancing at "gentlemen's clubs" in preparation for the work they will do after their acting jobs end. Both men and women have to pay for HIV testing every month. The fee comes out of their own pockets.

Another reason people said they worked in the porn industry was because they wanted fame and glamour. Porn production companies throw big parties and put on awards festivals similar to Hollywood's Oscars, like the flashy ceremony we saw at the Adult Entertainment Expo in Las Vegas. These can be alluring, especially for would-be actors and actresses who find it hard to break into Hollywood, much less win mainstream prizes for their performances. Porn, on the other hand, is very easy to break into and requires little or no acting skill. Abbott was told that if a woman is pretty, she can sign up with a producer and appear in a film within a few days.

Abbott found that people also like working in porn because of its flexible hours and sense of fun. "I just can't work in an office," an actress from Europe who was working in Los Angeles told Abbott. "I flip out — I get sick after two weeks. With [porn], I get to travel and have freedom. I got to come to the United States. I have enough money to take a vacation whenever I want."[4]

In addition, some actors and actresses said they like the work because it gives them a chance to act "naughty" and have a lot of sex. Most male actors cited "getting laid" as one of their main motivations. Some actresses also said this, and some added that porn sex makes the sex in their private life better because they learn more about their bodies. On the other hand, actresses said they didn't feel that the sex they had on the job was genuine. Actors, too, said they exaggerated their sexual pleasure while videotaping. They worried about losing their erections, and often had to masturbate between scenes to stay hard. Actresses said they could be working through a sex scene with an actor while equipment is being set up, and will usually moan only when the camera starts filming.

"You are playing to the camera," one woman said. She added that acrobatic sexual positions that look good on camera often make for sex that feels bad. Many performers reported feeling worn out and sore at the end of their workdays. When they got home, they didn't want to have sex with their partners.

Working in porn sometimes puts the workers' health at risk. Illegal drugs didn't seem to be a major problem: Abbott never saw workers using cocaine or heroin on production sets, though she did notice quite a bit of marijuana smoking. AIDS was a bigger danger. In 1998, several performers in Southern California were diagnosed as HIV positive. Since then, rules have become more strict, requiring actors and actresses to show documents proving they've tested negative for HIV during the past month. To protect against AIDS, condoms are supposed to be worn during sex scenes that include penetration. But when Abbott did interviews in 1998, she learned that condoms were hardly ever worn when the penetration involved vaginas. They were used mostly for anal intercourse.

Sexual harassment on the job was another problem. No actors or actresses said they had been forced to perform types of sex onscreen that they hadn't already agreed to. But many women said they had been pressured to have sex with directors. Younger actresses often did so because they thought they had to. It's hard to imagine this situation changing anytime soon.

And because porn is male dominated, it is particularly easy for new actresses to feel exploited. Film director and former actress Nina Hartley is reluctant to use teen performers because she believes they are immature. It's legal to work at the age of eighteen, but Hartley thinks that's too young. "Eighteen years old is when you should be focusing on intimate contact with a single person and trying to figure out who you are in your relationships," says Hartley. "Public sex isn't what you need to be doing at eighteen years old. I was twenty-three before I started."[5] Few teens have enough life experience to understand their bodies and sexuality, adds Hartley. No one "is drafting" them into porn, she notes. Still, she says, "I get angry at the business for blatantly taking advantage of someone young and stupid who wants to try something new."[6]

Most of the people Abbott interviewed called their work "stupid" and "ridiculous." Virtually no one thought that adult entertainment was serious art. "Porn sucks," complained one performer. In addition to feeling contemptuous of what they were doing for a living, actors and actresses had to worry about ending up unemployed. Because of aging and audiences' constant craving for fresh faces and bodies, performers lose their popularity after just a few years. As a result, most of the younger performers must make plans for what to do after they are pushed out of the industry. The replacement careers they aspired to included airline pilot and lawyer. Some wanted to go into business for themselves.

A common tale in the porn industry is that porn actors and actresses have had especially bad childhoods. Some performers told Abbott they had been sexually assaulted before they got into the business, and some said they thought the porn industry was a magnet for victims. But researchers who have looked for a connection between sexual abuse and sex work have not found one when they have interviewed "non-clinical samples" — workers who weren't already receiving therapy for psychological problems as a requirement for being in the studies. It seems wrong, then, to believe that most prostitutes, topless dancers and porn performers are in the business because they were sexually abused as children. Even so, porn performers often cite as gospel the idea that their field attracts people who have suffered abuse. This negative assessment may simply echo general misconceptions about porn and the porn industry. It may also be evidence that the performers feel bad about their jobs.

Another porn-related industry that employs women is "exotic" dancing, or stripping. In 2006, there were almost 2,800 strip clubs, or "gentlemen's clubs" in the US, 275 in Canada, 248 in Europe and 47 in Australia, according to Bernadette Barton, an American sociologist and women's studies professor. Barton spent five years interviewing dancers at these clubs for her book *Stripped: Inside the Lives of Exotic Dancers.*

Strip-club customers are almost all men, who pay to see women dancing nude or nearly nude. According to Barton's interviews, dancers' reasons for entering the field were similar to those that porn actors mentioned to Abbott. (In addition, it seems that many college students these days are stripping to help pay their tuition.) But dancers seem to have harder, riskier lives than hardcore porn actresses. Strippers complain of problems with alcohol and all sorts of illegal and prescription drugs. They tell of feeling physically and emotionally "burned out" after several months of club work. The extremely high-heeled shoes they dance in cause severe body and foot pain.

In addition, strippers are completely dependent on men's minute-to-minute approval in order to make a living. Good tips put them in a great mood, but bad tips or insults about their bodies can come the very next minute and make them feel terrible. They say the work is fun at first, but soon grows demeaning and exhausting. Another problem is high levels of stigma and social disapproval. The porn video industry is concentrated in small geographical areas: in suburban Los Angeles in the US, for instance, and in Montreal in Canada. But strip clubs are spread out, in hundreds of cities, and the work does not feel like a scene or industry where many other people are involved and accept each other's lifestyle. Furthermore, men in strip clubs are encouraged to get drunk; many then get rowdy and try to fondle the dancers or pick them up after hours. These problems don't exist in video making. Stripping seems like far harder work than porn — at least, as described by the actors Abbott talked with.

Abbott's study looked only at US performers, however. In other countries, particularly those with high poverty rates, young men and women are under much more pressure to work in porn than people in richer nations. Hungary is a good example. As we have already seen, the Hungarian porn industry is booming, with about a fourth of all porn videos produced in Europe made in and around Budapest. Most European porn stars are Hungarian. The reason for the strong porn industry in Hungary and other poor countries? Globalization. Like managers in other lines of business, pornographers are looking for countries with cheap labor and new markets to exploit.

In Hungary it takes only about $200,000 to make a high-end porn feature film — about half what it costs in Western Europe or the US. Hungary's official minimum wage is less than $100 a month and the average wage is only $220 — about $10 per workday. Yet by appearing in a porn film, a Hungarian can earn $50 to $5,000 a day, depending on whether the film is produced for the domestic market or for international distribution. Porn producers complain that in prosperous countries such as France, it is hard to find women who want to make porn. In Hungary, would-be actresses are turned away.

Economically depressed Brazil is also a popular production site for foreign porn producers. The Brazilian minimum monthly wage is about $165. Meanwhile, the going day rate there for a woman to appear in a porn scene is $400 (compared to up to $1,500 — and more for white stars — in Los Angeles).

Brazilian women performers usually have Latina features, or they are mixed Hispanic and black. Producers feel that Brazilian performers appeal to white American men's taste for the exotic. Performers whose physical features reflect a predominantly African heritage are seldom hired. Racism clearly plays a part in casting in Brazil, as it does in much porn.[7] Even in the US, black women usually earn half to three-quarters of what white performers are paid to make a hardcore film. The mostly white producers, directors, distributors and others who run the industry claim that black performers are less sexually desirable in the sexual marketplace than white performers.[8]

Hungarian porn performers are white, but they, too, are often portrayed in ways that make them seem inferior to viewers — even discounting the connotations of the sex scenes. The actresses' poverty and difficulties speaking English are often part of their "appeal."

Take *Global Warming Debutantes #4*, for example, directed by Ed Powers. In the video, he and a cameraman are driving around Budapest in a truck, supposedly trolling randomly for women they can talk into making a sex video. They quickly find a beautiful, leggy nineteen-year-old who seems happy to go to a house Powers has rented. There she disrobes, masturbates, and allows overweight, middle-aged Powers to fondle her while the camera rolls. She says she has never done anything pornographic like this before, and her supposed inexperience seems to be a big part of the video's appeal.

But who knows if she is telling the truth or if she is an experienced, professional performer? Much porn today claims to capture unvarnished reality, documentary style. But audiences never know to what extent "reality" itself is

The Many Lives of Linda Lovelace

The most widely read life story of a former porn actress may be four separate memoirs, all written by the same person. Her stage name was Linda Lovelace, and her claim to fame was her role in the notorious film *Deep Throat*. Released in 1972 in New York City, *Deep Throat* went on to gross $600 million internationally. Financially, it was one of the most successful motion pictures of any kind in the history of the world.

Lovelace was born Linda Boreman in 1948. She grew up in Yonkers, New York, the daughter of a New York City policeman and a domineering mother who believed in beating children to discipline them. Linda led what she later called a sheltered life. She first had sex at age nineteen and gave birth at twenty to a baby who she gave up for adoption.

When she was twenty-one she met twenty-seven-year-old Chuck Traynor, a small-time bar owner, pimp and pornographer. Traynor, whom Linda later married, put her to work as a prostitute and an actress in porn "loops," which were shown in peep-show booths and porn theaters. He also taught her to perform fellatio by taking the entire, erect penis into her mouth and down her throat without gagging. Because of this ability, Linda was "discovered" by a director who had acquired $23,000 of mob money to make a porn film.

The film's script centered around the star's noteworthy oral sex skills, and its title reflected the theme. Linda got about $1,200 to appear in *Deep Throat*. The money was actually paid to her husband.

Once released, *Deep Throat* became a sensation. Frank Sinatra went public with the fact that he had gone to see it. So did US Vice President Spiro Agnew, movie stars Warren Beatty and Shirley MacLaine, and writers Truman Capote and Nora Ephron. (Bob Woodward, one of the *Washington Post* journalists who uncovered the Watergate scandal, also saw the film. He called his secret Watergate informant "Deep Throat.")

In the first few years after *Deep Throat* was released, Linda published two autobiographies that celebrated pornography. In the first, *Inside Linda Lovelace*, she wrote that "I live for sex, will never get enough of it, and will continue to try

being staged. What does seem true, though, are offhand comments the woman makes as she agrees to do a porn performance. She tells Powers that she works as a saleswoman in a dress shop, full time, and makes only $150 a month —

every day to tune my physical mechanism to finer perfection... Nothing about sex is bad."[9]

She also tried to break into mainstream nightclub dinner theater and movie work. But she was not successful. By 1980, she had divorced, remarried and become a mother of two, a born-again Christian and a feminist. Now known as Linda Marchiano, she decided to tell her story a third time in the memoir *Ordeal*, co-written with journalist Mike McGrady.

In *Ordeal*, Marchiano denounced porn as a system of legalized sexual assault against women. She claimed she was forced to make films by Traynor, who threatened her with a weapon. "When you see the movie *Deep Throat*," she told the *Toronto Sun* in 1981, "you are watching me being raped... there was a gun to my head the entire time."

But *Ordeal* is full of contradictions. In other parts of the book, Marchiano wrote that she enjoyed performing in *Deep Throat* and that no one on the set made her do anything she didn't want to do. She wrote that Traynor assaulted her because he was jealous she was having a good time making the movie.

Ordeal was warmly embraced by anti-porn feminists, and so was Marchiano. She hit the lecture circuit, talking about the evils of porn for $1,500 per speech. In 1986 she testified before the US government's Meese Commission on Pornography, which was deliberately stacked with witnesses who criticized porn. Later she testified before the Minneapolis City Council when it was considering a law defining pornography as discrimination against women. And in 1986 she wrote her last autobiography, *Out of Bondage*, with an introduction by feminist Gloria Steinem. The book again portrayed the porn industry as a form of rape.

Marchiano never received a penny of royalties for her role in *Deep Throat*. She was plagued by financial hardship, and complained that after the excitement surrounding *Out of Bondage* died down, feminists lost interest in her and did not give her material help. She made a quiet attempt to re-enter the pornography industry as a magazine model but with little success. She developed serious health problems that got worse as the years went by, and in 2002, she lost consciousness while driving a car. She died as a result of the collision that followed.

like most other Hungarians. It is hard to know why such a depressing fact has not been edited out of this porn production. Perhaps US audiences are turned on by the woman's poverty and desperation.

They may also be attracted to her problems speaking English. This makes her seem mysterious, but also helpless and passive. Apparently there is an audience for such qualities. Here is how the porn DVD *Broken English*, produced in 2004, describes itself to prospective renters and buyers: "It doesn't matter how well they speak…only how well they FUCK! Sexy Euro-babes know how to make you understand!"

Helplessness coupled with economic hardship are also emphasized in the series *European Mail Order Brides*, made in 2003 and 2004. In the DVDs, the directors talk about how they advertised in a Budapest newspaper for women to marry them and return to the United States. The action opens with applicants who barely speak English coming for bride "interviews" and being told they can compete only if they give the directors oral sex. Some women seem shocked. Others talk about how poor they are in Hungary. "You want to go to America, don't you?" the directors continually cajole. Every woman eventually performs fellatio. Often the directors snicker, in English, about how naïve the girls are to believe this could get them to America.

Many porn performers in poor countries have no interest in American porn's lure of glamour, fame and sexual adventure. Instead, they want to make some quick capital, then use it to buy property or start a business. As one Hungarian actress said of her work in porn: "With the money I earned, I bought a three-bedroom apartment… I'm going to open a small grocery store, too."[10]

Chapter 9
Pluses Versus Pitfalls

Thirty years ago, Marilyn Fithian, a marriage counselor in the US, was trying to help her clients. Many had problems with their sexual relationships, and Fithian felt they needed tips about the mechanics of making love. She thought viewing XXX-rated materials could help, so she started sending couples to porn theaters. "They said they learned a great deal from the films," Fithian recalled years later when she spoke at a conference on pornography in California.[1] But the theaters were dirty and located in bad parts of town. They made people nervous. So Fithian started producing her own movies. They showed couples performing all kinds of sex acts, often with therapists commenting in the background on what was happening in the movie.

The films became popular with other therapists. They thought watching porn could make married couples happier. They also knew that a lot of children looked at porn on the sly — at their fathers' erotic magazines, for example. Many therapists thought this could be educational, too. Today many still do, and so do a lot of people who aren't therapists. "Porn remains about the only source of explicit information on sex for young people," Canadian artist and feminist Sara Diamond has commented. She remembers, as a child in the 1960s, "rifling secretively through *Playboy* at the corner drugstore."[2]

Many feminists agree that XXX materials can be educational. Karen Derzic and Alison Bodenheimer are co-owners of Girls Night In, a store in Pittsburgh that sells porn, sex toys and safer sex materials. They also host lectures and workshops for the community. "People — and women in particular — who are able to enjoy themselves and know that their desires are healthy and natural are happier, more empowered people," say Derzic and Bodenheimer. Pornography "can help people to realize that they are not the dirty perverts society told them they were."[3]

Compare those upbeat comments with darker ones made in 2003 by Canadian sex therapist and TV sex educator Sue McGarvie, who is based in Ottawa. "Explicit material for males between ten and seventeen is bad," McGarvie told a news reporter. She added that she was seeing "a bunch" of young men in therapy who were troubled by their exposure to pornography.[4]

McGarvie does not claim that porn leads boys and men to commit rapes or other crimes. As we've already seen, there's no proof for that theory. And there's no evidence that porn viewing alone causes psychological problems in adults or children. Of course, many people find porn offensive. But porn use has never been shown to cause depression, anxiety or any other clinical disorders, as they are referred to by mental health professionals.

So why are those young men going to see McGarvie and many other therapists throughout the world? What kinds of troubles are they having? Are young women experiencing difficulties, too? Does it make sense to single out porn as the cause? Or is porn just a symptom of deeper problems?

There's a lot of talk in the media lately about "pornography addiction." Men are going to therapy because they worry they are spending too much time and money on porn. They may be spending more than they can afford at strip clubs. More commonly, they hunch over computers for hours every day, surfing XXX sites and masturbating. They've stopped going out as much as they used to, cut down on exercising, sports and dating. If they already have partners or spouses, they are not paying as much attention to them as they used to. Or they don't feel as sexually turned on by their partners as they did before they started using so much porn. They want to cut down but they can't.

Does all this mean that overusing porn makes one like a slave to heroin or to three packs of cigarettes a day? Not according to Dr. Daniel Linz, Professor of Communication and Law and Society at the University of California, Santa Barbara, who finds that the ideas of "sexual addiction," "pornography addiction" and "on-line sex addiction" are "highly questionable." Linz adds that "scientists who have undertaken scientifically rigorous studies of exposure to sex materials report that despite high levels of exposure to pornography in venues such as the Internet, few negative effects are observed."[5]

New York City-based sex therapist Lenore Tiefer has patients who complain that they are obsessed with porn. She takes the problem very seriously but does not call these men addicts. "It's more that they've got a habit," she says. "Using pornography is just one of many, many things that people can do compulsively. Take eating cupcakes. Playing the clarinet. Or reading the *New York Times*"[6] — the thick, daily newspaper that takes hours to finish if you read every word.

"My patients who have problems with pornography were already suffering from conditions such as anxiety and depression. They started using the porn to soothe themselves," says Tiefer. "The same thing happens when people feel anxious or depressed and binge on, say, cupcakes. They eat too many and feel fat. Because they feel fat they don't want to go out and socialize. That makes them feel bad all over again and they try to comfort themselves by eating cupcakes. It becomes an endless loop." Another example Tiefer mentions is "the guy who can't help shutting himself in a room for hours every day and practicing the clarinet. He's got the same kind of habit as the porn users. Except maybe after several years he'll compose a brilliant song."

Unlike compulsive clarinet players, it's pretty hard for compulsive porn users to imagine doing anything noble with their habit. All they see in it is evil. Porn is still frowned on in society, so there is still a lot of shame attached to using it — more than overeating, and certainly more than spending hours with a musical instrument or a newspaper. Shame, Tiefer says, adds to people's sense that their porn use is a special sickness. An "addiction."

Tiefer treats compulsive porn users the same way she does patients with other troublesome habits. She encourages them to follow medical treatment for the clinical disorders — like anxiety and depression — that have pressured them into their problem behavior. And she helps them explore why they've been soothing themselves with one thing and not another: with the newspaper, say, and not cupcakes. Or if it's porn they've chosen, Tiefer asks them to look at their lives, present and past, and figure out what has made porn so appealing. "For example, someone who's had problems since childhood with a conservative father might have taken up porn as a way to rebel."

Tiefer also encourages her patients to think about why the particular style of porn they like seems so powerful. "Why are they getting so excited, for example, about the image or idea of group sex? Or rape? Or having a much younger partner?" Trying to figure out where these "deviant" fantasies come from in one's life is "like describing your dreams, then analyzing them," she says. "You realize that the fantasy has something to do with reality. That there's something about you in it."

But again, shame often gets in the way. "Mostly people get moralistic," says Tiefer. Instead of trying to figure out what the porn they're looking at says about relationships between men and women in society — and about their own desires and fears — they say, "I don't like this because it's bad, dirty."

That sense of badness and dirtiness is what gives porn its special, scary power in the public mind. "When people have problems with binging on cupcakes, no one talks about the evil of cupcakes or that they should be outlawed. They don't do that with newspapers, either, just because a small percentage of people spend too much time reading them," notes Tiefer.

On the other hand, she says, porn these days does have a unique quality: it's extremely easy to get, without even leaving home. Further, it has created something brand new: an endless, dazzling variety of erotic fantasies for people who are shopping around for ways to get aroused. From videos featuring slender, large-breasted blondes or fat, very pregnant black women to those that show nothing but feet, there is something for every sexual interest a person identifies with, and for many that he or she never imagined until running across them on a computer screen.

For many people, finding such images can feel liberating because they learn that others have the same fantasy. They no longer think of themselves as unique, or as perverts. But contemporary porn is also especially easy for troubled people to turn into a bothersome habit. "Because pornography is now in cyberspace and practically everyone has the Internet, almost everyone is scanning porn," Tiefer says. "Most will glance at it and move on to other things. A small proportion will develop the problems we're talking about."

New York City couples' counselor Meg Kaplan points out that, traditionally, many men have become involved in compulsive pastimes that take attention from their women partners and lead to relationship problems. Playing or watching sports, hunting and puttering in the garage are just a few. But a man's compulsive viewing of sexual materials can be much harder on his partner than other activities are. "She tends to feel she's competing sexually with the images of women in porn," Kaplan says. "That's what makes this Internet behavior different, and more troubling."[7]

Even when the female member of a couple is not bothered, the male may be, and that's as true for teens as for grownups. Canadian therapist McGarvie says porn can make her young male patients feel they are having "difficulties with intimacy… [When] your only images of women are of perfect women and women in adult movies, you have an unrealistic expectation of what real sex is like."[8]

Other therapists see another side to this picture. "Porn for boys can be something akin to the crushes that pre-teen girls get on movie stars," notes American child psychotherapist Sharon Lamb in a book about how to counsel children when they have concerns about sex.[9] "Girls can develop quite involved fantasies about their relationships with Orlando Bloom or Brad Pitt…only half remembering that it's only a fantasy…they are practicing romance." Boys, too, practice sex and sexual feelings toward a partner, writes Lamb, but they may do that with porn — which replaces reality with "a piece of paper or a photo on the screen…not a person in the flesh."

"In my experience," Lamb adds, "guys who have satisfying relationships with girls, who like them as people, and who've had nurturing family environments growing up — did you think I was going to say don't use porn? Ha! The truth is, that these kinds of guys use porn but are very aware that these women aren't real, still get enjoyment with real women, prefer real sex even though sometimes it seems too complicated and difficult, and realize a fantasy is a fantasy."

As with most of the important things in life, it takes experience to learn what "real sex" is like. Teenagers usually get very interested in it before they have had that experience. As a result, a lot of information gets passed around, some of it realistic but much of it not. When they first have sex, most people find it different from the glamour and perfection they've seen in Hollywood movies, on TV and in pornography. That's because the sex in these sources is performed, by paid actors and actresses who are following tight scripts that someone else wrote. Meanwhile, in the real world, every sexual experience unfolds differently and unpredictably.

First-time sex is no exception. Often it's full of heat. But it's also full of countless other things, and many can be surprising and confusing. Nervous behavior, intimate body odors, body hair, body fat, pimples, noises from belches and passing gas, kisses that land on the wrong spot, a partner who has trouble having an orgasm: the list goes on. Later, there are more real-life complications, like exhaustion after a hard day at work or anger over that morning's argument about money.

On the other hand, as partners learn about and adjust to each other's fantasies and needs — both sexual and non-sexual — the good parts of lovemaking get better. That's what relationships are about. Developing them is much more complex, fascinating and fun than anything that happens from merely studying the body parts and positions in a porn film.

But as Lamb suggests, watching porn can be pleasurable and educational for young people if they are mature enough to understand that what they are seeing is not real — and if they can call the shots about what they do and don't want to do with a partner. All that can be a tall order, however. A study done in Sweden and released in 2003 asked 1,000 women aged fourteen to twenty-four how being exposed to porn had affected them. About half were positive. One respondent, for instance, said porn gave her ideas about how to have sex and that it was a good influence. But many other young women said they didn't like porn. Their main objection: it pressured them into performing sex instead of feeling free to experience it on their own terms.[10] Another study of young women about the same age, also done in Sweden, found that those who'd seen porn were more likely to have had anal sex. Most didn't like anal sex, though.[11]

According to research in the US, abortion and pregnancy rates are decreasing among teens. The surveys also show that the current age that young people first have sex tends to be a little older than a generation ago. So porn doesn't seem to be turning adolescents into sex maniacs. On the other hand, it may be making the sex they do have less enjoyable. Ottawa sex educator Sue Johanson calls Canadian teens' involvement with anal sex "alarming." "The boys are demanding [it] and the girls are going along with it because they'll still be a virgin," she has said.[12] In New York City, therapist Lenore Tiefer is seeing increasing numbers of young women who complain about engaging in complicated acrobatic acts that aren't giving them much pleasure. "Oral sex on the first date is common," Tiefer says. "Anal sex is coming up fast. Meanwhile, there's a lot of faking of orgasms."

Tiefer believes young women are having sex they don't feel spontaneous about because they think — rightly or wrongly — that the men they meet expect this from watching porn. Even teenagers who are still having little or no sex say they're feeling negative effects. A southern California fifteen-year-old named Kirsten recently told the *Los Angeles Times* that porn, with its emphasis on perfect bodies, perfect faces and perfect Brazilian bikini waxes "causes girls to think they need makeovers. Like, I know people who are considering plastic surgery." Fourteen-year-old Amy added that because of porn, "You're supposed to have skinny thighs, [big breasts], flat stomachs." Scott, age sixteen, commented that porn conveys a message to young men like him that "you should be with these skinny blonde types." "And that sex should be unemotional," said seventeen-year-old Brad.[13] Anti-porn feminists used to warn that porn would turn men into raving-mad sexual predators. Now, writer Naomi Wolf wonders if it has had just the opposite effect: of lowering male interest in sex with real partners and their real cellulite and blemishes. For many men, Wolf has written, "real naked women are just bad porn."[14]

Many agree with Wolf. Pamela Paul is the author of *Pornified: How Pornography Is Transforming Our Lives, Our Relationships, and Our Families*. While researching her book, she hired a polling company to take a national US survey. The poll found that about half of American adults think porn changes men's expectations of how women should behave and look. Women believe this more than men do. A study of US teens' attitudes toward the Internet, released by the Kaiser Family Foundation in 2001, found that many teens believed porn could damage children and cause boys to develop bad attitudes toward the opposite sex. So, no matter what porn really does or doesn't do, people — at least in the US — tend to think it's harmful.[15]

But are porn's negative effects really so different from those caused by older, mainstream media?

Fashion magazines, television and Hollywood have for generations relentlessly promoted narrow images of what is supposed to be sexy. A recent poll of middle-aged and older Americans found that it's much more common — for both sexes — to get aroused by advertising, TV programs and mainstream movies than by porn.[16] Meanwhile, studies have shown that girls in the US commonly start dieting at the age of nine — long before they're exposed to hardcore pornography. In any case, women have never needed porn for ideas about how to stereotype themselves as sex objects. For years they've been tottering on painful high heels, cinching themselves into tight clothing and applying extravagant makeup. From time immemorial, they've been having sex they didn't enjoy in order to please men.

On the surface, the "pornification" that writer Pamela Paul complains about looks recent. But it's really a symptom of a much older problem: the idea that men have to be one way and women another. It's an ancient, undemocratic rule that's changing in fits and starts. Meanwhile, every single detail of life is being turned into a commodity — including our sexuality and parts of our bodies that the advertising industry never used to bother with. To feel desirable a generation ago, a young, urban woman had little choice but to spend money on a stylish haircut, a necklace, lipstick, a bottle of nail polish and a disposable razor. Now, to compete not just sexually but in the big-city job market as well, she must purchase salon pedicures, Botox injections, bikini or Brazilian waxes, and a nipple ring.

"Sex sells," the saying goes. But it's not really sex that's being marketed. Instead, it's fear: that if you don't buy products that make you look and act more feminine (or macho if you're male), you won't be beautiful or handsome or happy. Mix this fear with big media and mass marketing, and porn — lots of it — is bound to leak through the cracks.

Chapter 10
Censorship

Once upon a time, nannies were real people who worked in other people's homes and watched their children, using their five senses to keep the kids out of trouble. There are still plenty of human babysitters around, but lately they've been joined by cyber products like Net Nanny, a computer program that sells for $39.95. Once installed, according to its ads, Net Nanny "stops porn…from invading your child's computer, by filtering and blocking web content while they surf." Thousands of parents have bought the program to use in home computers. Other similar filters are being used by schools and public libraries. "Censorware" is big business because most people believe children need protection from porn — even though, as we've seen, there's no evidence that exposure to it affects kids differently than mainstream media does.

Adults have been trying for a long time to shield minors from words and images thought to be bad for them. The English language even has a special word for this: "bowdlerize." Thomas Bowdler, an English doctor, lived in the late 1700s and early 1800s and is famous for publishing the ten-volume *Family Shakespeare*. It contains many works by world-acclaimed playwright William Shakespeare. But, as Bowdler put it, he removed "those words and expressions...which cannot with propriety be read aloud in a family." In Shakespeare's play *Othello*, for example, the hero worries that Desdemona's "body and beauty" will distract him. In Bowdler, her body is deleted. "Kisses" are removed, too, and replaced by "sighs."[1] With modifications like these, Bowdler wrote, "a man could read aloud to his daughters with complete confidence" that their delicate thoughts would not be bruised.[2]

The Western concept of the tender-minded child goes back to ancient Greece and the philosopher Plato, who thought that young people needed special protection from wicked ideas. The Greek philosopher Aristotle agreed. "The unseemly remark lightly dropped," he wrote, "results in conduct of a like kind." In other words, children will do whatever bad things they hear about because they cannot help themselves. This ancient belief is so widespread today that for most people it seems like a natural fact of life.

As we have already seen, church and government officials a few hundred years ago often banned books and drawings containing sexual content because the same material also criticized religion and politicians. By the 1800s, though, very little porn did this directly. It existed mainly to get users sexually aroused. At first, pornography — and most other printed material — was expensive to make, so only the rich could buy it. But as printing became cheaper, access to all kinds of publications became more democratic. Porn was easier to get, even for those without much education or money.

In England and the United States, the upper classes thought they could handle "obscenity," which is another word for sexual materials that are considered unacceptable. But they worried that laborers, servants, women and — especially — children might see it, and that they could be easily swayed by bad ideas. All these groups needed protection from obscenity. In England, by the end of the nineteenth century, the courts had outlawed materials that might "deprave or corrupt those whose minds are open to such immoral influences and into whose hands a publication of this sort may fall." This meant that even if a thick book had just one passage involving sex, a child might read it — and that was enough to condemn the whole book.

As a result, works of great literature by authors such as Emile Zola and Gustave Flaubert were banned. The United States used the same law, and not just against publications. Starting in the 1870s, an official named Anthony Comstock worked with the postal service and seized anything considered "obscene" — anything deemed to violate community sexual morals — including birth-control medicines and devices that people were ordering through the mail. "Obscene" books were also illegal, including James Joyce's masterpiece *Ulysses*, which was banned until the early twentieth century. By then, a free-speech movement had developed in the US. It pointed judges to the First Amendment to the US Constitution, which defends freedom of speech, press, religion, assembly and petition — in general, allowing people to communicate what they want to without government interference. Using the First Amendment as a guide, a judge in the 1930s decided that *Ulysses* was not obscene because it was wrong to judge a publication by just a few passages. Instead, he said, a book should be looked at "as a whole." (Also in the 1930s, the law that banned sending birth-control information and devices through the mail was overturned. Even so, it was still illegal for people, even married couples, to own these materials. That law would not change until the 1960s.)

Television network and radio broadcasts are censored by the US government to remove "indecent" material. Hollywood movies are rated according to whether they are considered appropriate for children and adolescents. But by the late 1950s, a book, image or movie could no longer be outlawed in the US just because it might "deprave or corrupt" a weak-minded person. The "average person" — an adult — had to believe that his or her local community would find the whole product offensively sexual, or "prurient," as the law put it. But even if it *was* prurient, the work could be banned only if it was "utterly without redeeming social importance." The result? If a pornographer could convince a jury that a film full of, say, group and anal sex was even slightly educational, political or artistic, the work could not be judged obscene.

This new, narrower definition of obscenity opened the door to a flood of pornography and jump-started the enormous industry that exists today in the US. Pornography is not illegal in the United States. And today, there are virtually no restrictions on the printed word: anything sexual can be written about without the government stepping in. But when it comes to images such as photos and DVDs, local community standards for obscenity are different from one part of the US to another. The "average person" in San Francisco or New York City tends to be more liberal than the "average person" in Texas or Alabama. The federal government has prosecuted porn producers and distributors by pretending to be a mail-order customer and having porn sent from liberal communities to more conservative ones.

To protect themselves, the major porn producers have stopped making materials with themes they consider at risk of being judged obscene. These include scenes with people looking as though they're being forcibly raped and scenes involving sex with animals. Many other themes are legally acceptable in the US. Among these are anal sex and sex performed by people who are adults but who wear clothing or hairstyles to make them seem like children. In the US, the legal definition of a child is anyone from a newborn to a seventeen-year-old college student, and no one below the age of eighteen can legally appear in a porn production. This law has led to some bizarre situations, where teens goofing around with video and digital equipment have deliberately made porn of themselves — then have been charged with being child pornographers! And the government is trying to figure out how to tell the difference between digital images of real children in sexual poses and "morphed" images — those showing adult porn performers whose faces and bodies have been digitally altered to make them look like children. These pictures might be morally repulsive, but in the US, child pornography is illegal because it is a record of a real child being exploited. If there is no victim, there is no crime.

Laws are different in other countries. Some have traditionally been more liberal; Denmark, for example, has no obscenity rules at all. In Japan, many comic books (called "manga") show hardcore sex and violence, but they are legal and widely read by people of all ages, children included. In the United Kingdom, on the other hand, obscenity laws are stricter than in the US. A product in the UK can be banned even if it has no sex in it. Books containing violence have been outlawed. So was a publication that described people using illegal drugs — the government thought it might encourage readers (especially younger ones) to take drugs themselves. Until recently it was illegal to bring "indecent" materials into England, including books about homosexuality. But the UK recently joined the European Union (EU), a political, economic and social organization of twenty-five European countries. EU member states are not allowed to block products coming from other members. As a result, pornographic materials that used to be banned are now imported to England.

In Canada, materials can be outlawed not just if they have sex in them but also if they include crime, horror, cruelty or violence. As a result, many books and movies that are legally viewed in the US, even by children, are banned for people of all ages north of the border. The situation gets even stricter when violence combines with sex, as it does in porn styles such as S&M. In the province of Ontario, all movies must be reviewed by the Ontario Film Review Board, not just porn. Cuts are usually made by manufacturers before they submit the movie to the board. But there is a black market in Canada for original versions of censored films.

As discussed in Chapter 6, Canadian bookstores specializing in lesbian and gay products, such as Little Sisters in Vancouver, have been especially hard-hit by government restrictions. It is illegal in Canada to show adult actors and actresses pretending to be younger than eighteen, and to use computers to morph images of adults so they will look like minors. (In 2005, legislation was introduced into the US Congress to create a similar law.) In Canada, New Zealand and Australia, it is illegal to write about children having sex, even if it is fiction. Civil liberties activists in Australia have criticized the statute, pointing out that a fifteen-year-old girl who keeps a diary describing sleeping with a teen boyfriend could be arrested. She could be locked up to protect society from a person who encourages sex with children. But that person herself would be a child. The logic makes no sense.

It makes no sense, either, to insist that people younger than eighteen get hurt by looking at pornography, because there is no proof for that claim. But it doesn't matter. As one US psychiatrist told a court, laws against porn should be on the books because children who read porn are "protected… by the knowledge that it is…disapproved" of by parents. According to this "do as I say, not as I do" argument, kids need to hear adults say that porn is bad — even if those same adults seek out porn and know that children do.

But why, exactly, is it bad?

Because it's "immoral," according to many traditional religions. Yet laws in democratic societies are supposed to guard citizens' safety, not dictate religious beliefs or morality. As Pierre Trudeau said in 1967 when he headed Canada's justice department: "There's no place for the state in the bedrooms of the nation." Trudeau was speaking back then of the need to abolish bans on homosexual behavior. But he could just as easily have been talking about porn. Laws against pornography cross a moral line into the bedroom, say many civil libertarians. But few will speak up loudly; they worry that if they do, they'll be accused of not caring about children. Or, perhaps worse these days, of being unpatriotic.

In 2005, a twenty-eight-year-old man from Florida, Chris Wilson, was running an amateur site where people paid a few dollars each month to post homemade porn photos, mainly of girlfriends and wives. Soldiers stationed in Afghanistan and Iraq tried to join, but Wilson's system could not process their credit cards. He came up with an offer for the soldiers: if they sent pictures from overseas proving they were in the military, they could access the site for free.

Digital pictures poured in from places like Baghdad. Some were humdrum shots of life in the barracks and Middle Eastern street scenes. Others were chilling. They showed the uncensored horrors of war: charred, bloodied and blasted bodies, including those of children and other civilians. Wilson named the site www.nowthatsfuckedup.com.

When the international media started reporting about the site in 2005, many people — even those who oppose the US invasion of Iraq and Afghanistan — were offended by what they felt was the tastelessness of the pictures of dead bodies. They liked the amateur porn raunch even less. As for the US military, officials expressed disgust but said Wilson had a right to free speech. But soon the district attorney in Wilson's county in Florida was charging him with hundreds of counts of obscenity — not for the military images, supposedly, but for the homemade porn. Wilson was jailed, released on bail, then jailed again. Most charges were eventually dropped, but in order to go free, he had to agree to shut down his site.

Wilson was defended by a lawyer representing a local chapter of the American Civil Liberties Union (ACLU). This national US organization is famous for defending First Amendment rights when they involve political speech. Other arts and civil liberties groups, such as PEN, a writers' organization, and library associations in many countries, defend the legal right to make and distribute porn that tickles the edges of obscenity law. They get very nervous when the phrase "child pornography" comes up, however. And governments know this — especially nowadays.

Within weeks of Al Qaeda's September 11, 2001, terrorist attacks on the United States, the US passed a set of laws called the Patriot Act. It gives police and prosecutors rights they never had before. For example, investigators can search people's homes without letting them know. They can rifle through personal financial and computer records, check on purchases from bookstores, and even monitor the materials an individual has checked out of a library. Many Americans are so troubled by the Patriot Act that hundreds of communities have passed resolutions condemning it. But the government continues to defend it, saying that porn is one reason the act is needed.

In 2004, US Attorney General John Ashcroft testified before Congress that the Patriot Act had helped catch two Internet child pornographers. It had enabled investigators to ask an Internet service provider for the names of the criminals, then get a warrant to search their houses. At first, Ashcroft's testimony got face-value press. But later, some news sources found out that investigators knew who the pornographers were and where they lived before they used the Patriot Act. They had learned the old-fashioned, constitutional way: by talking to a child victim and to an adult who had witnessed wrongdoing. The Patriot Act had little or nothing to do with solving the crime. But the government's "protecting kids from harm" argument gave the new law great press.

Amid this flood of language about danger and war and the safety of children, young people are on their own when it comes to getting the facts they desperately need to know. Teen pregnancy rates in the US are fifteen times higher than in Japan and much higher than in Scandinavia, the Netherlands, Great Britain and Italy. Researchers believe that a major cause of the problem is that in the US, public-school sex education courses, when they exist at all, refuse to recognize that teens are having sex and instead promote "abstinence," encouraging teens not to have sex before marriage. This leaves only one place to go for realistic information: the Internet. It is an enormous library with almost limitless resources, including many on sexuality. Websites like teenwire.com and gURL.com give frank advice about relationships, rape, AIDS, masturbation, orgasms, birth control, and other topics that teens must know about to stay healthy, safe and happy in the modern world. But while trying to keep minors away from porn, censorship threatens to block educational sites like these.

Young people know this is happening from their own experience. A 2001 study done in the US found that most fifteen- to twenty-four-year-olds had gone online for health information. Almost half who did so were using the net to look up information about pregnancy, birth control, HIV/AIDS and health issues related to sexual activity. But their searches were often frustrating. Many said they had been blocked by filters.[3] Another study backed up that claim with statistics. Using several censorware filters that libraries and schools often employ to screen out porn, researchers keyed in terms such as "safe sex," "condom" and "gay." The filters blocked as many as one of every two health sites.[4]

Despite these findings, a law called the Children's Internet Protection Act was passed in the US in 2000 and is still in effect. American public schools and libraries usually receive money from the federal government, and the Internet Protection Act says that to get this funding, they must install NetNanny-like software. This cleanses public places of porn, health information — and even science, academic discussion and literature. Filters have been found to block websites for the American Association of University Women, the Yale University Graduate Biology Program, the classic children's poem "The Owl and the Pussycat," and the award-winning novel *Bastard Out of Carolina*. One filtering system, used by the state of Utah in all public schools and some libraries, blocked the US Declaration of Independence, *The Adventures of Sherlock Holmes* — and the plays of William Shakespeare.

But things could be worse. In 1996, the US Congress passed the Communications Decency Act (CDA), making it a crime to send anything "obscene" or "indecent" over the Internet to someone younger than eighteen. Under the CDA, those teen-oriented sexual health sites would not just be blocked — they'd be shut down. A mother could be arrested for emailing her seventeen-year-old college-student son or daughter information about sex or birth control. Moderators of a teen chat room could be prosecuted if, during a discussion about censorship, an eighteen-year-old member were to post the comment, "Fuck the CDA."

The CDA was ruled unconstitutional in 1997. Meanwhile, though, censorship is thriving in the lower-tech world of the printed book. In the United States, parents are the group of adults most likely to try to remove a book from schools and public libraries. They worry about the racism discussed in works like *Huckleberry Finn*. They fret about curse words in *Crazy Lady!*, a prize-winning, young adult novel about a teenager's friendship with an alcoholic woman. Parents especially disapprove of sex and sexuality in works such as *It's Perfectly Normal* (which deals with nudity, abortion and gay sex), or *It's So Amazing! A Book about Eggs, Sperm, Birth, Babies and Families*. Of the top ten censored books in the US in 2005, seven had sexual themes. The federal government does not enforce censorship of children's books in schools and libraries, but local efforts have a nationally chilling effect. In 2007, for instance, US children's librarians refused to order *The Higher Power of Lucky*, an award-winning book for nine-to-twelve-year-olds. The librarians feared problems from parents because it contains the word "scrotum."[5] A widely banned book can spell trouble for a publisher. It can be easier to avoid controversy and canceled orders by sticking to bland topics.

Meanwhile, porn is everywhere; kids simply cannot be shielded. Even the most restrictive Internet filters fail to catch about 10 percent of pornographic websites,[6] and as we have seen, many young people seek out porn. Given these realities, censorship seems useless. But there is a better alternative: instruction in "media literacy." Literacy means the ability to understand and use information, instead of information using you.

Worldwide, some countries teach media literacy classes in public schools. Until recently, media literacy instruction has concentrated on how to evaluate what's hype versus what's true on the Internet, in the news and in ads. (For a great example of how fashion advertising subtly tampers with teen girls' bodies, see www.demo.fb.se/e/girlpower/retouch/index.html.) But now, media literacy advocates are urging that porn be added to the curriculum. Using skills gained through media literacy lessons, a young person encountering porn could evaluate it by asking questions such as: Why are these pictures being shown to me? Is what I am seeing a true and realistic image of what sex is like? Why are other people drawn to these images? What important things are not shown? What are the circumstances that led these individuals to be filmed or photographed? Could an adult help me better understand what I'm seeing?[7]

This approach is far more useful than censorship. It is about broadening and deepening perceptions, not narrowing them — which is impossible to accomplish anyhow when it comes to sexual imagery. In the old days, when porn was only available in books, magazines and videos, it was hard enough to control. Today, however, it's digital. It is no longer a physical object, and governments cannot destroy megapixels. The Internet is breathtakingly cheap, convenient and hard to regulate. Porn nowadays is too democratic to be censored.

Besides, as University of Texas art historian John Clarke points out, censorship contains its own, built-in contradiction. As long as we try to fence off sexual representations from the rest of life, they will continue to exist and — given the intense commercialization and advanced technology of contemporary life — increase beyond our wildest imaginings. Many people hate this fact. Many more feel confused by it, even troubled. But like it or not, the act of giving pornography a name has made it part of our culture. "We have named porn," says Clarke. "And it's not going to go away."[8]

Child Pornography

As arguments rage about whether hardcore porn is good for the world or bad, one genre seems beyond controversy: kiddie porn. Most adults are deeply offended by the idea of children acting sexually for others' pleasure. Common wisdom has it that those who make or even look at such images should be severely punished. It's a black-and-white issue. Or so the thinking goes — until people like British musician Pete Townshend, Canadian resident Andrzej Mikuta and some teenagers from the US state of Virginia and the Canadian province of Quebec are put in the mix.

Townshend, former lead guitarist for the rock band The Who, was arrested in England in 2003 in an Internet child-porn case. He claimed he came across illegal pictures as he was randomly surfing the Web while researching a book about child sexual abuse and Internet child porn. His name was placed on a sex offenders registry for five years. Like many men caught with child pornography that they have downloaded from the Internet, Townshend had no record for molesting children.[9] Nor did he have a history of involvement with child porn. He was caught along with several hundred other people around the world in an international online investigation called Operation Ore. Virtually everyone arrested was male. Very few had any criminal history related to the Ore charges. Most had apparently wandered into kiddie-porn sites while Internet surfing. Some had looked once and never returned. Others had downloaded a few images that remained in their hard drives even if they had deleted them.

In 2000, Andrzej Mikuta was accused of making child porn after he took pictures of his four-year-old son naked. Charges were eventually dropped, but not until after Mikuta underwent psychological testing to see if he was a pedophile. (He wasn't.) The Virginia teens — two high school girls — photographed each other wearing only underpants, then emailed the pictures to their boyfriends in order to be "flirtatious." They were slapped with felony charges of production and dissemination of child pornography. (The charges were dismissed but the girls were banned from participating in school activities.) In a similar case in 2005, a thirteen-year-old girl in Mont Lanier, Quebec, emailed nude photos she took of herself to a boy she was friends with at school. He forwarded them to some of his friends. Law enforcement authorities arrested them, and though criminal charges were not laid, an Ottawa detective noted that the teens had made and distributed child porn. The student's school principal was disturbed that the girl who took and emailed the pictures of herself "seemed to think her behavior was 'normal.'"[10]

These cases were all related to digital images on the Internet. But a generation earlier, the 1970s was a bumper decade for child pornography in films and magazines, which were produced in Europe and usually featured teenagers under eighteen. The United States outlawed the importation or sale of this material in 1977. By the late 1980s, the government was practically the only producer and distributor of child porn in the US. Using photos from the old European publications, federal authorities made their own magazines and tried to entice pedophiles to order them through the mail so they could be arrested. The government and media often claimed during this time that kiddie porn was a multi-billion-dollar-a-year business involving millions of children worldwide. In fact, according to researchers who investigated these claims, there was almost no commercial market for child pornography. Their research showed that at most, a few thousand children internationally were being used in homemade material that pedophiles did not sell but, instead, mostly traded with each other.[11]

Things changed with the arrival of computer technology. Early bulletin board systems (BBSs), newsgroups, encrypted sites and the World Wide Web allowed child porn to make a comeback online. In 2006, a Texas congressman told a US House of Representatives hearing that child pornography is a "twenty-billion-dollar-a-year business." That frightening claim was repeated by the *New York Times* and other media. It was quickly debunked by the *Wall Street Journal* as having no foundation in fact.[12]

Even so, child pornography appears to be a real problem in cyberspace. Pennsylvania State University historian Philip Jenkins has done careful investigation into use of the Internet by pedophiles.[13] Jenkins did his work between about 1995 and 2000. He estimates that during that time 50,000 to 100,000 die-hards across the world were trading child porn with each other on the net. Mostly they recycled old pictures from the 1970s magazines and films. But some images appeared to be "sex tourist" shots made by men visiting Asian or Latin American countries. Children in these nations tend to be poor, so it is easy to recruit them as models. And some pictures contained strong evidence that fathers were molesting their own children. Victims ranged in age from babies to adolescents.

Many of the message boards Jenkins found were based in Japan, Russia and other Eastern European countries. The person posting the picture, the server, the picture site where other users could locate the image and the site with the access password — could each be in a different country. This has made law enforcement extremely difficult. So has the fact that — as was the case in the 1970s and 1980s — very little money is involved in today's hardcore child pornography trade. Rather than being sold, most of the material is exchanged for free among pedophiles. Jenkins believes that most of the users know how to mask their identities online, and that they understand far more about computer technology than the law enforcement authorities. So far, it has been impossible to catch the vast majority of people who upload and download kiddie porn.

Still, Jenkins thinks online child pornography can be reduced. In general, he is against government control of Internet access and believes it is misguided to target people who accidentally run into child porn while surfing the net. At the same time, he believes that message boards and newsgroups that distribute the child porn should be shut down, country by country. He thinks this will be very hard, though, because poor countries will always be tempted to make money by hosting servers that are used for child porn.

Jenkins also wants all countries to fix the minimum age for appearing in porn at sixteen years old. This is an important change, because the legal age currently varies from country to country. In some countries, like the US, the legal age is eighteen, but in others it is only sixteen. As a result, images on many sites are legal in some countries but illegal in others, and it is very difficult to coordinate law enforcement internationally. In addition, while it is illegal in the US for children to pose provocatively, even when they are fully clothed, in other countries the children must be nude in order for the images to be banned. And in some nations, they can be nude and provocatively posed, as long as no actual sexual touching is shown. As a result of these differences — as this writer discovered while researching legal porn for this book — it is shockingly easy to run across material on the net that is classed as child porn in the US but is legal in other nations.

Jenkins would like to see more logic brought to bear on these and other situations related to child pornography. He is against prosecuting parents who take pictures of their children with no evidence of sexual motives, or children who willingly use themselves as models and share the photos and videos with peers. Finally, Jenkins believes that researchers should be able to view child pornography. Otherwise, the government will decide behind closed doors what is illegal porn and what isn't.

This is dangerous, because — in the US, at least — it's clear the government may be making mistakes. There, sexual images of children are legal if they are images of adults that have been altered by Photoshop or if they are completely computer-generated, involving no real children. But how to tell if an image is real or "virtual"? In 2006, a judge in Massachusetts ruled in the case of a man who was arrested after authorities found a kiddie porn image on his computer. To prosecute, the Justice Department wanted to use as an expert a college professor who had developed a program that he claimed could tell if an image was real or not. Lawyers for the accused man, however, learned that the program made many mistakes. The FBI then said its own agents could distinguish between real and Photoshop-altered images simply by looking at them. The judge disagreed. "It may be possible to digitally create or manipulate photographs in a manner the naked eye cannot detect," she wrote in a legal ruling. "The government has not shown otherwise."[14]

Obviously, the government needs input and oversight from citizens, some of whom are experts in the workings of the net and could teach law enforcement about how cyberspace works with relation to child porn. Government secrecy is never healthy for democracy, even when democracy is trying to protect kids.

Chapter 11
The Future of Porn

If hardcore pornography refuses to go away, what will happen to it in the future? Will new technologies change its form and how we experience it? Could more democratic production and distribution create material that shows what desire is like for women and for others who traditionally have been porn's objects instead of its creators? Will XXX-rated materials be used not just for profit or individual pleasure, but for the social good as well? And if this happens, would sexual imagery become so everyday, so acceptable, that it no longer seems separate and shameful?

Would porn stop being porn?

That possibility might sound like science fiction. But politically and technologically speaking, there is evidence that porn continues to evolve by leaps and bounds. Here's the latest: it is being used to save rainforests. And it's moving from mere pictures and voices into the realm of interactive touch. If the trend continues, porn may bring people together, not just as sex partners but as activists — even the people who nowadays sit alone by their computer screens, masturbating to the old-fashioned material.

The Fuck for Forest website was created in 2004 by a

young Norwegian couple. They call it an "ecological porn site" run by "concerned humans" who "use their sexuality and love to direct attention to and collect money for the earth's threatened nature." Fuckforforest.com recruits volunteers to donate sexual photos and videos of themselves. It charges $15 a month to view this mostly amateur material, then sends the profits to rainforest conservation and reforestation efforts in Central and South America. In its first year, the website collected $100,000.

"Dildonics" are electronic devices — sex toys — that are controlled by a computer. "Teledildonics" is technology that allows two people to masturbate together, with the sensation of touch transmitted over a data link even if they are thousands of miles from each other.

The Sinulator is one teledildonics device. It includes a transmitter, a vibrator and a receiver. The men's version is a sleeve that the penis can be slipped into. The women's is a dildo for insertion into the vagina. Customers can visit the company's website, sinulator.com, to choose a name for their toy. Once the toy is named, anyone can choose it on their computer's control panel and operate it.

The men's toy measures the speed and force of each thrust and communicates this information to the software. The software turns the measurements into vibration and pulse at the receiver end. A man can be thrusting in France while a woman in the US is being penetrated.

Regina Lynn, a columnist with the US magazine *Wired*, says that women like teledildonics because partners have to instant message their instructions to each other. That forces them to send clear, verbal cues about their likes and dislikes, and ask what the other person does or doesn't want. In teledildonics porn, women's desires are just as active and important as men's. "The attention, the wordplay, the sensual imagery... It's like starring in your own erotic story," Lynn has written. "The better you communicate, the better your Sinulator experience will be."[1]

Steve Rhodes is president of Sinulate Entertainment; he says he has sold thousands of Sinulators since 2002. When partners are separated for long periods of time, the Sinulator can create a feeling of togetherness. He adds that "the Iraq war [was] kind of a boom for our company,"[2] as it separated troops from their civilian partners.

But Sinulators are for couples who know each other before they connect their toys. Another company, HighJoy.com, sells a teledildonics experience for people who want to start brand-new relationships. They register with the organization and make contact on the Internet. They can start off by typing messages to each other. Then, if they want the relationship to turn sexual, they shift into teledildonics.

In the online magazine *Salon*, writer Anna Jane interviewed twenty-eight-year-old Dani, who said she started using HighJoy because she likes sex, but found it hard to meet men in Los Angeles, where she lived. Dani wanted to search for partners who lived farther away. Through HighJoy, she found a man named David, who lived in Spain.

"I feel closer to David than I do to anyone else I've chatted with, because I've let him be intimate with me," Dani told Jane.[3]

Jane had teledildonic sex, too. She hooked up with a young man in Florida. The two chose not to post their pictures or talk over the phone. Instead, they simply chatted back and forth in a chat room for a while.

"To my astonishment," writes Jane, "there was something weirdly sweet about the whole thing. Unlike porn, this made me the recipient of all the attention. It was kind of touching that someone — even a stranger — wanted to pleasure a real me in lieu of getting off on Jenna Jameson. At the same time, I didn't feel as physically and emotionally exposed as I would be having sex with a man I'd just met if he were actually in my bed."

Future porn likely will also involve fictional beings especially tailored to real, individual humans, says Julia Heiman, director of the Kinsey Institute for Research in Sex, Gender and Reproduction at Indiana University in the US. She expects this to happen by 2016. "There is a possibility of developing erotic materials for yourself that would allow you to create a partner of certain dimensions and qualities, the partner saying certain things in that interaction, certain things happening in that interaction."[4]

Could a sex robot be developed? Something like the one that Jude Law portrayed in the 2001 film *AI: Artificial Intelligence*?

Carl DiSalvo, a doctoral student at Carnegie Mellon University's School of Design, in Pittsburgh, has helped design a robotic device that imitates the warmth and feeling of a hug. It could be adapted for sex, he says. Other researchers say machines will be developed that will create sexual stimulation without the genitals being touched. Marvin Minsky, a professor emeritus at MIT in Boston, has studied artificial intelligence since 1951. He said devices like this would trigger an actual physical response from the brain, making the whole experience feel just like sex — without any bodily "mess" or health risks. "It's bound to happen," Minsky says. He speculates it could take two or three decades. "But if the game [industry] people got involved in some underdeveloped country that didn't have any laws against it, it could all happen twice as fast."[5]

Some researchers worry that virtual experiences might hurt people by isolating them. A simulated relationship "decreases what is essential in human life, which is sociability — one's capacity to relate to other people," said John Gagnon, a long-time researcher and author of books about sexuality.[6]

Others are more upbeat. "Cybersex gets blamed for a lot of things, including social isolation, infidelity and divorce. It's a temptation previous generations of lovers didn't have to face, and it's technology, and therefore it's scary for a lot of folks," writes *Wired* writer Regina Lynn.[7] But teledildonics "has as much potential to bring people together as it does to drive people apart."[8]

Arguments like these will probably go on endlessly, according to pornography researcher Joseph Slade. And the controversy will just make porn more popular. "Each generation 'reinvents' sexuality and gender," Slade writes, "using evidence from laboratories but also documents from popular culture. For all their public assurance, scientists and doctors understand relatively little about the biological basis of human sexuality, still less about gender, and even less about psychological triggers of arousal. Is sexual attraction biologically determined, or is it socially constructed? Does pornography mimic 'natural' desire, or fabricate it? It is here, at the juncture of uncertainty and ignorance, that pornography seems most menacing and most entertaining."[9]

In other words, as humans we always want to know more about ourselves than we can know. Our questions and boundless curiosity about what makes people tick sexually are what give porn its great power. It has a strength rivaled only by religion — which we also use to answer questions about life that ultimately can't be answered. But religion traditionally has been in the moral mainstream, while porn is at the margin. Now, the Internet has pushed porn into the church of public life through the sanctuaries of home computers and cheap, uploadable digital devices — allowing people to experience sexual images privately, record them privately and upload them to the world. Eventually a point could come, says Fenton Bailey, "where pornography is so commonplace that it is rendered completely unsecret and without taboo." It was invented a century and a half ago as a category to regulate people's behavior. But regulation now doesn't work well. Which means that porn as an idea is losing its meaning.

So will porn just stop existing?

Hard to tell, Bailey writes. "Taboos and prejudices can be eroded but are rarely erased." Even so, he adds, the sense of porn as something shameful and rebellious seems to be fading.[10]

But whether or not we hold on to the old idea of porn, art will always depict sex and sexual fantasy, no matter what technology we use. Sex, after all, "both challenges and affirms the power of art; it is the bottom line, the ultimate proof that representation has the power to disturb, to ravish, to arouse, to console."[11]

Surely we will always have pictures, sounds, music,

Breast Implants and Other Porn Extremes

In stag films from ninety years ago, the women have natural
pubic hair and breasts. That's also true for films made during
porn's "golden years" in the 1970s. Plastic surgery had been
developed by then, but actresses stayed away from the knife.
Shaving was minimal.

On the other hand, performers in many productions from
the 1980s have big, silicone implants that have pumped their
cup size to DD or beyond. And porn videos from the 1990s
show women with bare pubic areas. Today, porn actresses have
completely bald genitals, particularly in North America. Men,
too, are hairless, not just on their genitals but also on butts,
chests, legs and shoulders. Some sport rings in their penises.
Women may have pierced nipples. In Europe, however, many
performers keep their pubic and even underarm hair. They tend
to have natural breasts. And they rarely display rings in their
breasts or genitals.

What is all the injecting, piercing and waxing about?
Waxing in particular makes many women outside the porn
industry nervous because they think porn actresses do it so men
can fantasize about having sex with little girls. Siliconed
breasts, of course, do not look like a child's flat chest. Yet
they're on the same performers who have the bald genitals. It's
confusing.

Porn researcher Joseph Slade has a theory about these and
other extremes that porn performance imposes on bodies. He
mentions two things that seem to be part of porn's definition
and which bring enjoyment to people who use porn. One is
technology. The other is bodily control. In many ways, the two
cannot be separated.

While traditional Western culture sees sex as a means of
reproduction, Slade notes that porn is virtually never about
making babies. Reproduction is avoided by "the money shot" —
when the man removes his penis from the woman's vagina just

before he ejaculates. Oral sex and anal sex do not cause pregnancy either, and they are extremely popular in porn. Slade points out that when porn was first defined in the nineteenth century, information about birth control was included as part of the definition.

Birth control involves chemicals and devices. These are technology. If we accept Slade's definition of technology as "any means by which a species alters itself or its environment," then, as he puts it, "pornography is a technology of pleasure."

From time immemorial, humans have been fascinated at how they can change their moods, work habits, social relations and bodies by using technology. Grape and other plant juices were transformed into wine and liquor to create the alcohol "buzz" that enhanced religious insight and sociability. Ochre, kohl and tattooing turned body parts into message boards about membership in a tribe or readiness for sex. Trains closed the distances between people. Telephones served the same function.

Technology often frightens people even as it fascinates and seduces them. When the locomotive passenger train was in its early days, for instance, many passengers came down with inexplicable neck and back pains, often becoming paralyzed. Injuries could never be found, though, and eventually the "illness" died out. Likewise, when the telephone was first invented, many people denounced it as dangerous to girls because seductive male voices could now enter a young lady's house without her parents' knowledge.

Today, technology continues to intersect with bodies to send erotic messages and bring people together. Contemporary porn shows spectacles of physical control that look much like sports or dance. Like ballet performers or gymnasts, porn stars are often heavily made-up, extremely costumed, and quick to contort into positions that are impossible for most people. In all these activities the body is like a machine, a piece of high technology. In this context, enormous breasts and genital hairlessness may also be a way of showing mastery over the body.

These physical changes are also a reflection of the technological changes in porn production over the past generation. Slade points out that back in the 1970s, the age of natural breasts and hair, porn sex occurred on giant theater screens where it was easy to see little details. But when porn went to video, the screen became tiny. Perhaps breasts had to be pumped up and genitals shaved so that audiences could see things better. And perhaps this new beauty standard has even affected people who are not porn performers. Today, many women outside the industry have surgery to enlarge their breasts, and genital waxing has entered the fashion mainstream.

Slade finds that the trend toward anal sex in porn may also be a reflection in part of modern society's interest in "gender-bending." This sort of penetration has traditionally been thought of as "unnatural" because it is not a means of reproduction. Now, penetrating a woman anally is a dramatic denial of her traditional reproductive role. As a form of birth control and a negation of traditional gender identities, anal sex may seem "artificial" or technological.

According to Slade, the technological side of porn is one source of its tremendous appeal.[12] Yet people are also frightened by technology, and with good reason. After all, it can and has been used to do truly horrible things. The Nazi mass-murder gas chambers and ovens were high tech for their time. So was the A-bomb. But technophobia can also be irrational.

This conflict is like the Greek myth about Icarus. He wanted to fly — something humans cannot do naturally — so he strapped on wings to artificially extend his body's power. He flew and flew, and came too close to the sun. He caught fire and crashed from the sky.

Porn, too, can be as unnatural to people as having wings. It can be just as tempting — and equally scary.

movies and sculpture. Who would not want these marvels? But it's up to us to decide whether we want the images we see in fashion, television, Hollywood, pop music — and yes, in our "adult entertainment" — to be "pornified" or not.

We will not get rid of graphic, raunchy sexual imagery by making people ashamed of their passion for it. We won't make a dent with censorship. As we have seen, these efforts only create passion and more porn.

If we really want to depornify, we will have to accept — or better, celebrate — that interest in sex and sexual imagery is part of the human condition. In addition, we will have to accept the seductive concepts of democracy and citizenship. After all, what could be a bigger turn-on than a world where everyone has the right to express his or her sexuality, without having to act out someone else's because of poverty, oppression or ignorance? What could be more exciting than sex education that helps young people know who they are — not by adopting stereotyped identities such as stud, hottie or good girl, but by understanding themselves as community members and complicated individuals? And what could be more alluring than citizens helping to make a society where big, profit-driven corporations don't decide how to use technology (including the Internet) but instead, people do?

In a world like that, we would not let the government censor sexual imagery. Nor would we pay much attention to Net Nannies, anti-porn preachers and porn "addiction" counselors. Instead, we would see a riot of new movies, pictures and sounds, not to mention touches and even robots. All this would be very different from what we have now. It might take a different name. Or we might laugh at the sadness of history, and just to be funny, call it porn.

Landmarks in the History of Pornography

1524 Pietro Aretino's *I Modi* is published in Italy, first as a series of engravings of men and women having sex, and later with a ribald sonnet accompanying each picture.

1564 The Catholic Church issues the Index Librorum Prohibitorum, or Tridentine Index of prohibited books. It is updated every fifty years until 1948. It is finally rescinded in 1965 after blacklisting more than 4,000 works.

1655 Jean L'Ange and Michel Millot are convicted in Paris of publishing *L'École des Filles, ou la Philosophie des dames* (The Girls' School, or the Philosophy of Women).

1660 John Garfield of England is imprisoned for writing *The Wandering Whore*.

1712 Massachusetts, then an English colony, passes a law against obscene writing and pictures.

1780s Advertisements for imported erotic novels appear in newspapers in New York and Massachusetts.

1789 In France, freedom of speech is established by the Déclaration des droits de l'homme et du citoyen. But two years later, legislation is passed outlawing "public assaults on the modesty of women by indecent action," the sale of "obscene pictures," and "the corruption of young persons."

1791 Adoption of the United States Bill of Rights, including the First Amendment, prohibiting government interference in speech or other forms of expression.

1802 Great Britain's Society for the Suppression of Vice and for the Encouragement of Religion and Virtue is established to "check the spread of open vice and immorality, and more especially to preserve the minds of the young from contamination by exposure to the corrupting influence of impure and licentious books, prints, and other publications."

1810 Isaiah Thomas prints the first American edition of John Cleland's *Fanny Hill* in Worcester, Massachusetts.

1821 Two booksellers are prosecuted in Boston for selling *Fanny Hill* on grounds of obscenity.

1842 The Tariff Act, the first federal obscenity law in the US, bans the importation of obscene materials into the country.

1848 The first graphically sexual daguerreotype is produced, depicting a couple engaged in intercourse.

1857 The word "pornography" appears for the first time in English. The Tariff Act of 1842 is amended to prohibit erotic daguerreotypes.

1868 British magistrate Benjamin Hicklin issues a ruling making it illegal to publish any material that has even a short paragraph that might corrupt the most vulnerable members of society — anyone whose minds were "open to immoral influences." The so-called Hicklin decision is the court response to an 1857 act in England forbidding the sale and distribution of "obscene libel." The logic of the Hicklin decision will be used for many years to prosecute obscenity in the US.

1873 Anthony Comstock (1844-1915) successfully lobbies federal anti-obscenity statutes through Congress, which passes the Comstock Act. It outlaws the production, sale, distribution or possession of printed material, devices and medicines deemed "obscene." These include not only sexually explicit writing and pictures, but contraceptives, drugs to cause abortion, and information about how to prevent or end pregnancy. Comstock founds the New York Society for the Suppression of Vice.

1876 The Comstock Act is amended to give the US Post Office power to censor.
In Canada, the Postal Service Act of 1875 and the Customs Act of 1879 prohibit the sending or importing of obscenity through the mail, and in 1892 the publishing of obscene books for profit is banned. Obscenity is defined along the lines of England's 1868 Hicklin case.

1882 Boston bans Walt Whitman's *Leaves of Grass*.

1890 Tolstoy's *Kreutzer Sonata* is banned from the mail under the Comstock Act.

1896 Thomas Edison first exhibits a movie projector to the public, showing his film *The Kiss*, which shows a man and woman kissing.

1907 A film showing sexual intercourse is made in Vienna.

1908 The mayor of New York City closes all cinemas on grounds of immorality.

1909 The New York Board of Motion Picture Censorship, now the National Board of Review, is established to approve new films before they are released to the public. Similar review boards in other states follow in subsequent years.

1914 New York City nurse and contraception advocate Margaret Sanger first uses the phrase "birth control" in her journal *The Woman Rebel*. The New York City postmaster bans the journal as obscene under the Comstock Act. Sanger is indicted for nine violations of the law. She flees to England.

1915 *A Grass Sandwich*, the first surviving US hardcore (stag) film, is shot in New Jersey.

1916 Margaret Sanger is indicted for sending diaphragms through the mail. She is arrested in 1917 for opening the first birth control clinic in the country.

1917 Clara Bow appears nude (with her breasts and genitals shielded) in the movie *Hula*.

1920 A judge in *Halsey v. New York Society for the Suppression of Vice* rules that a book should be evaluated as a whole, not just using isolated passages. He also rules that the books must be evaluated by qualified critics rather than by anti-vice workers.

1927 Mae West is sentenced to ten days in jail for doing an "obscene" dance in the play *Sex*, which she wrote.

1928 D.H. Lawrence has his novel *Lady Chatterley's Lover* printed privately in Italy. Soon pirated editions spread through Europe and the United States.

1930 Theodore Dreiser's *An American Tragedy* is declared obscene in Boston under the Hicklin principle. Massachusetts also condemns *Lady Chatterley's Lover*.

1933 A judge overturns the Hicklin principle in *United States v. One Book Called Ulysses* by declaring that the book, by James Joyce, must be considered as a whole.

1934 Hollywood adopts a strict censorship code formulated by the Catholic "Legion of Decency."

1935 The US Treasury Department burns a seized copy of *Ecstasy*, a Czech film starring Hedy Lamarr, which shows her swimming nude in a brief scene. The first issue of the nudist magazine *Sunshine and Health* is published, showing naked people.

1942 Betty Grable poses for the most famous pinup of World War II, and has her legs insured for $1 million.

1947 Launch of *Vice Versa*, the first US lesbian magazine.

1948 Alfred Kinsey and colleagues publish *Sexual Behavior in the Human Male*.

1953 Kinsey and colleagues publish *Sexual Behavior in the Human Female.*
The first edition of *Playboy* magazine is released, featuring a nude photograph of Marilyn Monroe.

1957 New York State Court of Appeals clears a nudist colony film for exhibition on grounds that nudity is not obscenity. In *Roth v. The United States*, the Supreme Court rules that a work can be deemed obscene only if it offends community standards and if it is "devoid of serious literary, artistic, political or scientific value." The ruling opens the floodgates to porn in the US.

1959 *Lady Chatterley's Lover* ruled not obscene in a New York legal case. *The Immoral Mr. Teas*, directed by filmmaker Russ Meyer, is released.

1960 *Lady Chatterley's Lover* is ruled not obscene in the UK.

1961 Henry Miller's book *Tropic of Cancer* (Paris, 1934) is published in the United States.
The birth control pill is introduced.

1964 Comedian Lenny Bruce is tried for obscenity, but a federal court in Illinois throws out his conviction. The FBI launches an investigation of obscenity in the lyrics of "Louie Louie," by the Kingsmen, but gives up when no one can agree on the meaning of anything in the song.

1966 The Supreme Court reverses Massachusetts' finding that *Fanny Hill* is not obscene.
Hollywood rescinds its 1934 censorship code and replaces it with PG, R and X ratings.

1968 Swedish film *I am Curious Yellow* plays in the US.
John Lennon and Yoko Ono appear nude on the album cover of *Two Virgins.*

1969 Denmark lifts all restrictions on pornography for people older than 16, and sex crimes decrease.

1970 The President's Commission on Obscenity and Pornography recommends abolishing restrictions on the distribution of porn to consenting adults. *Penthouse* magazine's first centerfold shows pubic hair on its monthly "pet."

1971 The first commercially successful gay hardcore film, *The Boys in the Sand*, is released.

1972 *Deep Throat* opens in New York City and becomes an international sensation. *The Devil in Miss Jones* is released. *Behind the Green Door* is released. Hollywood star Burt Reynolds poses nude for *Cosmopolitan* magazine.

1973 Charlene Webb shoots *Goldenrod*, the first hardcore feature film made by a female director. The American Psychiatric Association drops homosexuality from its list of mental disorders. Abortion is legalized in the United States.

1974 *Dyketactics*, the first explicit film shot by a lesbian, is released.

1979 Women Against Pornography is founded in New York City.

1981 AIDS is recognized as a fatal disease, which enhances porn as a "safe sex" alternative.

1982 Consumer camcorders are introduced, enabling just about anyone to make his (or her) own porn video. The amateur genre is born.

1983 Dial-a-porn begins, with recorded sexually explicit messages. Catharine McKinnon and Andrea Dworkin write the Minneapolis ordinance banning pornography.

1984 Minneapolis city council passes the McKinnon/Dworkin ordinance, which is then immediately vetoed by the mayor. Other radical feminists write a similar ordinance for Indianapolis. First annual Adult Video News Awards Ceremony, dubbed "the Oscars" of the adult entertainment industry.

1985 The Indianapolis ordinance is overturned on grounds that it violates the First Amendment.

1986 Attorney General Edwin Meese impanels a commission to overturn findings of the 1970 Presidential Commission on Obscenity and Pornography.

1988 A California State Supreme Court decision defines porn performers as actors rather than prostitutes, making it unnecessary to make porn videos in secret.

The director of the Contemporary Arts Center in Cincinnati is arrested for exhibiting the homoerotic and sadomasochistic photographs of Robert Mappelthorpe.

A federal judge in Florida finds a record album by rap group 2 Live Crew obscene.

1992 Canada adopts a strict antiporn law at the urging of McKinnon and Dworkin. Canada Customs seizes *Bad Attitude*, published by a Boston lesbian collective, then confiscates books by Dworkin.

Madonna publishes the photo-book *Sex*. A federal judge overturns the Florida courts' ruling that the 2 Live Crew album is obscene.

1994 Patti Reagan Davis, daughter of former president Ronald Reagan, poses nude for *Playboy*.

Commercialization of the Internet begins, with a total of 10,000 websites and 10,000 news groups online.

1995 The US Senate passes the Communications Decency Act (CDA) aimed at controlling porn on the Internet. A Supreme Court decision defines even digitally constructed images of fully clothed children as child pornography, if these images can be said to be sexually appealing to someone.

1996 A Court of Appeals finds the CDA's ban on Internet indecency unconstitutional. Internet providers develop filters such as Net Nanny for parents to use to screen sites for children.

1997 The US Supreme Court upholds a lower court ruling that the CDA is unconstitutional.

The number of Internet sex sites reaches 10,000.

1998 Kenneth Starr releases a pornographic report on Bill Clinton's sexual encounters with Monica Lewinsky, leading to impeachment proceedings against the president.

The US Federal Communications Commission is told it cannot ban journalists from using the word "penis" on the air.

Sex and the City debuts on TV. It focuses on the sex lives of four women in New York City, and often touts anal sex.

1999 The adult video industry produces 10,000 new cassettes.

Private Media becomes the first adult entertainment company to be traded on the NASDAQ stock market.

2004 *How to Make Love Like a Porn Star*, by porn superstar Jenna Jameson, is published to favor-able mainstream media reviews and prominently displayed at bookstores.

2006 Thirteen-year-old Masha Allen, who was adopted by a pedophile and whose image is all over the Internet, speaks to the US House subcommittee on oversight and investigation in Washington. The so-called Masha's Law is introduced in the US Senate. It would allow vic-tims over eighteen to sue anyone who buys, sells or distributes pornographic pictures taken of them when they were minors.

Notes

Chapter 1

1. Henry J. Kaiser Foundation, "Generation Rx.com: How Young People Use the Internet for Health Information" (Menlo Park, CA: Henry J. Kaiser Foundation, 2001). Available at www.kff.org/entmedia/20011211a-index.cfm. The Kaiser Foundation is a US-based organization that investigates public health issues.
2. John Schwartz, "Forsaking TV for Online Games and Wanton Web Sites," *New York Times*, March 29, 2004.
3. Feona Attwood, "Marketing Sex to Women," *Sexualities*, Vol. 8, No. 4 (2005), 393.
4. Carey King, "Pole-dancing, 'stripping' – even lap dancing – are the hot new trends in sensual fitness," *New York Newsday*, May 25, 2006, B4.
5. Pamela Paul, *Pornified: How Pornography is Transforming Our Lives, Our Relationships, and Our Families* (New York: Times Books, 2005).

Chapter 2

1. Lynn Hunt, ed., introduction to *The Invention of Pornography: Obscenity and the Origins of Modernity, 1500-1800* (New York: Zone, 1993), 10.
2. All references to currency are in US dollars.

Chapter 3

1. Eric A. Zimmer and Christopher D. Hunter, "Risk and the Internet: Perception and Reality," in *Citizenship and Participation in the Information Age*, eds. Manjunath Pendakur and Roma Harris (Aurora, Ontario: Garamond Press, 2002). See also Dick Thornburgh and Herbert S. Lin, *Youth, Pornography, and the Internet* (Washington, D.C.: National Academies Press, 2002), available at www.nap.edu/books/0309082749/html/; Maryclaire Dale, "One Percent of Web Deemed Pornographic," *USA Today*, November 15, 2006, available at www.usatoday.com/tech/news/techpolicy/2006-11-15-web-pornography_x.htm.
2. Dan Kindlon and Michael Thompson, *Raising Cain: Protecting the Emotional Life of Boys* (New York: Ballantine Books, 2000), 205.
3. Marty Klein, telephone interview with author, June 2006.
4. Joseph Slade, telephone interview with author, February 2006.
5. Ibid.

Chapter 4

1. Linda Conrad, *Between Strangers* (New York: Silhouette Books, 2004), 133–37.
2. Nielsen//NetRatings, June 2000, cited in "Sizing up the Cyberporn Industry," www.msnbc.com/modules/SmutSultans/Industry/default.asp
3. "Websense Research Shows Online Pornography Sites Continue Strong Growth, Increasing By Over 1.5 Million Since 2000, as Internet Porn Vendors Pioneer New Technology," April 4, 2004, press release, www.websense.com/global/en/PressRoom/PressReleases/PressReleaseDetail/?Release=040405588. Websense, Inc. is a company hired by many businesses to track Internet use by employees.
4. Thornburgh and Lin, *Youth, Pornography and the Internet*.

5. Trevor Hayes, "Online Sex Sells at Internext," *Las Vegas Review Journal*. Available at www.reviewjournal.com/lvrj_home/2001/Jan-06Sat2001/business/15174717.html.

6. "Internet Porn Fuels Cybersex Addiction," reprinted by Zogby International. Available at www.zogby.com/soundbites/ReadClips.dbm?ID=12322.

7. SexTracker.com, cited in *Free Speech Coalition White Paper 2005: A Report on the Adult Entertainment Industry*, www.freespeechcoalition.com/whitepaper05.htm. The Free Speech Coalition is the legal arm of the adult entertainment industry in the US.

8. Michael Rubin, comScore Media Metrix, personal communication with author.

9. Sonia Livingstone and Magdalena Bober, "UK Children Go Online: Final report of key project findings" (Economic & Research Council, London School of Economics), April 28, 2005. Available at www.children-go-online.net/.

10. Rachel O'Connell et al., "Emerging Trends Amongst Primary School Children's Use of the Internet," Cyberspace Research Unit at the University of Central Lancashire, Preston, UK, February 2004. Available at www.uclan.ac.uk/host/cru/publications.htm.

11. "National Survey of American Attitudes on Substance Abuse IX: Teen Dating Practices and Sexual Activity," National Center on Addiction and Substance Abuse at Columbia University, August 2004. Available at www.casacolumbia.org/support-casa/item.asp?cID=12&PID=82.

12. "Alberta boys lose track of porn viewing," The Associated Press, February 22, 2007. Available at www.msnbc.msn.com/id/17284408.

13. Henry J. Kaiser Foundation, "GenerationRx.com."

Chapter 5

1. Ron Langevin and Suzanne Curnoe, "The use of pornography during the commission of sexual offenses," *International Journal of Offender Therapy & Comparative Criminology*, Vol. 48, No. 5 (2004), 572–86.

2. U.S. Commission on Obscenity and Pornography, Report of the U.S. Commission on Obscenity and Pornography (Washington, D.C.: U.S. Government Printing Office, 1970).

3. H.B. McKay and D.J. Dolff, "The Impact of Pornography: A Decade of Literature," *Working Papers on Pornography and Prostitution* (Ottawa Department of Justice) 13 (1985).

4. Albert Bandura, Dorothea Ross and Sheila Ross, "Imitation of Film-Mediated Aggressive Models," *Journal of Abnormal and Social Psychology* 66 (1963), 3–11.

5. Edward Donnerstein and L. Berkowitz, "Victim reactions in aggressive-erotic films as a factor in violence against women," *Journal of Personality and Social Psychology* 41 (1981), 710–24.

6. Neil Malamuth and J. Check, "Sexual Arousal to Rape and Consenting Depictions: The Importance of the Woman's Arousal," *Journal of Abnormal Psychology* 92 (1980), 55–67. See also Neil Malamuth and J. Check, "The effects of aggressive pornography on beliefs of rape myths: individual differences," *Journal of Research in Personality* 19 (1985), 299–320.

7. D. Linz, N. Malamuth and K. Beckett, "Civil Liberties and Research on the Effects

of Pornography," cited in P. Suedfeld and P. E. Tetlock, eds., *Psychology and Social Policy* (New York: Hemisphere, 1992), 149–64.

8. P. H. Gebhard et al., *Sex Offenders: An Analysis of Types* (New York: Harper and Row, 1965).

9. L. Conyers and P. D. Harvey, "Religion and Crime: Do they go together?" *Free Inquiry,* Vol. 16, No. 3 (1996), 46–48; M. J. Dougher, "Assessment of Sex Offenders," cited in B. K. Schwartz and H. R. H. Cellini, eds., *A Practitioner's Guide to Treating the Incarcerated Male Sex Offender* (Washington D.C.: U.S. Department of Justice, National Institute of Corrections, 1988), 77–84.

10. M. J. Goldstein and H. S. Kant, *Pornography and Sexual Deviance: A Report of the Legal and Behavioral Institute* (Berkeley: University of California Press, 1973). See also M. M. Propper, "Exposure to Sexually Oriented Materials among Young Male Prisoners," Technical Report 8, Commission on Obscenity and Pornography (Washington, D. C.: U.S. Government Printing Office, 1972).

11. Judith Becker and Robert Stein, "Is Sexual Erotica Associated with Sexual Deviance in Adolescent Males?" *International Journal of Law and Psychiatry,* Vol. 14, No. 1-2, 85–95.

12. Berl Kutchinsky, "Pornography and Rape: Theory and Practice? Evidence from Crime Data in Four Countries Where Pornography is Easily Available," *International Journal of Law and Psychiatry,* Vol. 4, No. 1-2 (1991), 47–64.

13. Milton Diamond and Ayako Uchiyama, "Pornography, Rape and Sex Crimes in Japan," *International Journal of Law and Psychiatry,* Vol. 22, No. 1 (1999), 1–22. Available at www.hawaii.edu/PCSS/online_artcls/pornography/prngrphy_rape_jp.html.

14. Ibid.

15. For more information on this issue, see Alison King, "Mystery and Imagination: The Case of Pornography Effects Studies," cited in Alison Assiter and Carol Avedon, eds., *Bad Girls and Dirty Pictures: The Challenge to Reclaim Feminism* (Boulder, CO: Pluto Press, 1993), 57–87; Marcia Pally, "Standard Deviation: Research Literature on Sexually Explicit Material and Social Harms," cited in *Sex and Sensibility: Reflections on Forbidden Mirrors and the Will to Censor* (Hopewell, NJ: Ecco Press, 1994), 25–61.

Chapter 6

1. Robin Morgan, "Theory and Practice, Pornography and Rape" (1974), from Robin Morgan, *The Word of a Woman: Feminist Dispatches 1968–1992* (New York: W.W. Norton and Co., 1992), 88.

2. Lisa Palac, "How Dirty Pictures Changed My Life," cited in Adele M. Stan, *Debating Sexual Correctness: Pornography, Sexual Harassment, Date Rape, and the Politics of Sexual Equality* (New York: Delta, 1995), 249.

3. Ellen Willis, "Feminism, Moralism and Pornography," cited in Stan, *Debating Sexual Correctness,* 43.

4. Gloria Steinem, "Erotica and Pornography: a Clear and Present Difference," *Ms.,* November 1978. Reprinted in Laura Lederer, ed., *Take Back the Night: Women on Pornography* (New York: William Morrow, 1980), 35-39.

5. Diana Russell, *Against Pornography: The Evidence of Harm* (Berkeley, CA: Russell Publications, 1993), 3. See also www.dianarussell.com/pornography.html.

6. B. Ruby Rich, "Anti-Porn: Soft Issue, Hard World," in Patricia Erens, ed., *Issues in Feminist Film Criticism* (Bloomington: Indiana University Press, 1990), 410.

7. Judith Levine, "Perils of Desire," *Village Voice Literary Supplement*, March 1985, 1, 12–15.

8. Andrea Dworkin, *Letters from a War Zone* (Brooklyn: Lawrence Hill Books, 1993), 119.

9. Catherine A. McKinnon, "Pornography: An Exchange," cited in *New York Review of Books*, Vol. 41, No. 5, March 3, 1994. Available at nybooks.com/articles/2310.

10. Richard Roeper, "Do the Films Exist, or Are They Just Another Urban Legend? S'nuff Already," *Chicago Sun-Times*, March 21, 1999, 402.

11. David Kerekes and David Slater, *Killing for Culture: Death Film from Mondo to Snuff* (London: Creation Books, 1996).

12. Laura Lederer, "Snuff films just another handy myth to exploit," *Toronto Star*, March 5, 1999, Entertainment section.

13. Susie Bright, susiebright.blogs.com/susie_brights_journal_/2005/04/andrea_dworkin_.html. Reprinted in the introduction to *The Best American Erotica of 2006*, ed. Susie Bright (New York: Touchstone, 2006).

14. Lisa Duggan, "Censorship in the Name of Feminism," *Village Voice*, October 16, 1984.

15. Feminists for Free Expression, www.ffeusa.org/html/mission/index.html.

16. Lisa Palac, "How Dirty Pictures Changed My Life," 249.

17. Ann Snitow, "Retrenchment Versus Transformation: The Politics of the Anti-Pornography Movement," cited in Varda Burstyn, ed., *Women Against Censorship* (New York: HarperCollins, 1985), 119.

Chapter 7

1. Timothy Egan, "Wall Street Meets Pornography," *New York Times*, October 23, 2000. Available at www.nytimes.com/2000/10/23/technology/23PORN.html.

2. Paul Fishbein, interview, "Porn in the USA," *Sixty Minutes*, November 21, 2003. Transcript available at www.cbsnews.com/stories/2003/11/21/60minutes/main585049.shtml.

3. Tristan Taormino, "Political Smut Makers," *Village Voice*, June 14–20, 2006, 137.

4. For more about Mason, Taormino, Hartley, Angel and many other women in the porn industry, see Carly Milne, ed., *Naked Ambition: Women Who are Changing Pornography* (New York: Carroll and Graf, 2006).

5. Frank Rich, "Naked Capitalists," *New York Times*, May 20, 2001.

6. Ibid.

7. Dan Ackman, "How Big is Porn?" Forbes.com, May 25, 2001. Available at www.forbes.com/2001/05/25/0524porn.html. See also Emmanuelle Richard, "The Naked Untruth," May 23, 2002. Available at www.alternet.org/story/13212/.

8. Scott Hetrick and Dana Harris, "Vid Revs Generate Steam for Porn Biz," *Daily Variety*, December 14, 2005, 26.

9. David Cay Johnston, "Indications of a Slowdown in Sex Entertainment Trade," *New York Times*, January 4, 2007, C6.

Chapter 8

1. Christina Noir [pseud.], telephone interview with the author, December 2005.
2. Carly Milne, ed., *Naked Ambition*, 91–92.
3. Sharon Abbott, "Motivations for Pursuing an Acting Career in Pornography," in Ronald Weitzer, ed., *Sex for Sale* (New York: Routledge, 2000). See also Abbott's doctoral thesis: "Careers of Actresses and Actors in the Pornography Industry," Indiana University, 1999.
4. Abbott, "Careers of Actresses and Actors in the Pornography Industry," 124.
5. Robert J. Stoller and I. S. Levine, *Coming Attractions: The Making of an X-Rated Video* (New Haven, CT: Yale University Press, 1993), 152.
6. Ibid., 166.
7. Information about the porn industry in Hungary and Brazil is from Katalin Szoverfy Milter and Joseph W. Slade, "Global Traffic in Pornography: The Hungarian Example," cited in Lisa Z. Sigel, ed., *International Exposure: Perspectives on Modern European Pornography, 1800–2000* (Piscataway, NJ: Rutgers University Press, 2005); Allyson Vaughan, "Pornography: Hungary Exports Sex and Videotapes," *The Ottawa Citizen*, January 4, 1997.
8. Information about the earnings of black women performers in the US is from Mireille Miller-Young, "Hardcore Desire: Black Women Laboring in Porn – Is it Just Another Job?" *ColorLines Magazine*, Winter 2005.
9. Joe Bob Briggs, "Linda's Life: A Sad Story, and Its Impact on Us All," *New Republic*, April 25, 2002; Linda Marchiano, *Ordeal* (New York: Kensington, 2006 [1980]).
10. Natasha Singer, "Blue Danube – The Story of Budapest's Booming Export: The Skin Flick," Nerve.com, February 25, 2001, cited in Szoverfy Milter and Slade, "Global Traffic in Pornography: The Hungarian Example."

Chapter 9

1. Marilyn A. Fithian, "Importance of Knowledge as an Expert Witness," cited in James D. Elias et al., eds., *Porn 101: Eroticism, Pornography and the First Amendment* (Amherst, NY: Prometheus, 1999), 122.
2. Varda Burstyn, ed., *Women Against Censorship* (New York: HarperCollins, 1985), 52–53.
3. The Thomas Merton Center, "The Naked Feminist – And a Local Business Empowering Women," www.thomasmertoncenter.org/The_New_People/July-August2004/naked_feminist.htm.
4. Georgie Binks, "How the Internet is Killing Real Relationships," Viewpoint, *CBC News*, November 3, 2003. Available at www.cbc.ca/news/viewpoint/vp_binks/20031103.html.
5. Daniel Linz, "Response to Testimony before the United States Senate, Subcommittee on Science, Technology, and Space of the Committee on Commerce, Science and Transportation on The Science Behind Pornography Addiction," 2004. Available at www.freespeechcoalition.com/dan_linz.htm.
6. Leonore Tiefer, interview with the author, February 2006.
7. Meg Kaplan, interview with the author, September 2006.
8. Binks, "How the Internet is Killing Real Relationships."

9. Sharon Lamb, *Sex, Therapy, and Kids: Addressing their Concerns through Talk and Play* (New York: W.W. Norton, 2006), 188.

10. Christina Rogala and Tanja Tyden, "Does Pornography Influence Young Women's Sexual Behavior?" *Women's Health Issues,* Vol. 13, No. 1 (2003), 39–43.

11. Tanja Tyden et al., "Improved Use of Contraceptives, Attitudes Toward Pornography, and Sexual Harassment among Female University Students," *Women's Health Issues,* Vol. 11, No. 2 (2001), 87–94.

12. Angela Mangiacasale, "Teens Have Sex Early, Often and Unprotected," *The Ottawa Citizen,* September 22, 1999.

13. Shawn Hubler, "Just the Facts of Life Now," *Los Angeles Times,* April 23, 2005.

14. Naomi Wolf, "The Porn Myth," *New York Magazine,* October 20, 2003. Available at www.newyorkmetro.com/nymetro/news/trends/n_9437/.

15. Henry J. Kaiser Foundation, "GenerationRx.com."

16. *AARP the Magazine,* "Sexuality at Midlife and Beyond: 2004 Update of Attitudes and Behaviors" (Washington, D.C.: American Association of Retired Persons, 2005).

Chapter 10

1. Michael Macrone and Tom Lulevitch, *Naughty Shakespeare* (New York: Gramercy Books/Random House, 2000). For a sample of unexpurgated Othello versus Bowdlerized Othello, see "Old Books, New Pedagogy: Special Collections and Archives in the Curriculum," an electronic version of an exhibition in Olin Library, Wesleyan University. Available at www.wesleyan.edu/libr/schome/exhibit/Teaching/Pedagogy/seven.htm.

2. Thomas Bowdler, cited in Marianna Beck, "The Pornographic Tradition," in James Elias et al., eds., *Porn 101* (Amherst, NY: Prometheus, 1999), 386.

3. Henry J. Kaiser Foundation, "GenerationRx.com."

4. Henry J. Kaiser Foundation, "See No Evil: How Internet Filters Affect the Search for Online Health Information" (Menlo Park, CA: Henry J. Kaiser Foundation, 2002).

5. Julie Bosman, "With One Word, Children's Book Sets Off Uproar," *New York Times,* February 18, 2007, 1A, 31A.

6. Henry J. Kaiser Foundation, "See No Evil."

7. Thornburgh and Lin, eds., *Youth, Pornography and the Internet,* 247–48.

8. John Clarke, interview, *Pornography: The Secret History of Civilisation,* DVD, directed by Chris Rodley and Dev Varma, 2000.

9. For more on the growing number of people caught with Internet porn who have no history of molesting children, see J. Paul Fedoroff, "The Paraphilic World," in Sharon B. Levine, ed., *Handbook of Clinical Sexuality for Mental Health Professionals* (New York: Brunner-Routledge, 2003), 333–56.

10. Toby Cohen, "The Arrests of Several West Quebec High School Students on Child Porn Charges Illustrate the Dangers that Await Online," *Ottawa Sun,* December 17, 2005.

11. Lawrence A. Stanley, "The Child Porn Myth," in *Cardozo Arts and Entertainment Law Journal,* Vol. 7, No. 22 (1989).

12. Carl Bialik, "Measuring the Child-Porn Trade," *Wall Street Journal,* April 18, 2006.

13. Philip Jenkins, *Beyond Tolerance: Child Pornography Online* (New York: New York University Press, 2001).
14. Declan McCullagh, "Police blotter: Detecting computer-generated porn?" C/net News.com, January 3, 2007, news.com.com/Police+blotter+Detecting+computer-generated+porn/2100-1030_3-6145563.html.

Chapter 11
1. Regina Lynn, "Ins and Outs of Teledildonics," *Wired*, September 27, 2004. Available at www.wired.com/news/culture/0,65064-0.html.
2. Adam Tanner, "Future Sex: Gizmos, Robots," *Reuters*, April 17, 2006.
3. Anna Jane, "Single, White with Dildo," *Salon*, August 29, 2005. Available at dir.salon.com/story/mwt/feature/2005/08/29/teledildonics/index.html.
4. Adam Tanner, "Future Sex."
5. Ibid.
6. Ibid.
7. Regina Lynn, "Ins and Outs of Teledildonics."
8. Regina Lynn, "Build Your Sex Dream Machine," *Wired*, June 3, 2005. Available at www.wired.com/news/culture/0,1284,67719,00.html.
9. Joseph Slade, *Pornography in America: A Reference Handbook* (Santa Barbara: ABC-CLIO, 2001), 7.
10. Fenton Bailey, "Let it all hang out," *The Guardian*, October 8, 1999. Available at film.guardian.co.uk/Feature_Story/interview/0,,90016,00.html.
11. Joseph Slade, *Pornography in America*, 20.
12. Joseph Slade, telephone interview with the author, February 2006.

For Further Reading

Elias, James et al, eds. *Porn 101: Eroticism, Pornography and the First Amendment.* Amherst, NY: Prometheus Books, 1999.

Gever, M. et al., eds. *Queer Looks: Perspectives on Lesbian and Gay Film and Video.* New York: Routledge, 1993.

Jenkins, Philip. *Beyond Tolerance: Child Pornography on the Internet.* New York: New York University Press, 2001.

Slade, Joseph W. *Pornography in America: A Reference Handbook.* Santa Barbara, CA: ABC-CLIO, 2001.

History and Analysis

Bailey, Fenton and Randy Barbato, dirs. *Pornography: The Secret History of Civilization.* Video (2 parts), 2005.

Hunt, Lynn. *The Invention of Pornography: Obscenity and the Origins of Modernity 1500-1800.* New York: Zone, 1993.

Kendrick, Walter. *The Secret Museum: Pornography in Modern Culture.* New York: Viking Press, 1987.

O'Toole, Laurence. *Pornocopia, Updated Edition: Porn, Sex, Technology and Desire*. London: Serpent's Tail, 2000.

Sigel, Lisa Z. *International Exposure: Perspectives on Modern European Pornography, 1800–2000*. Piscataway, NJ: Rutgers University Press, 2005.

Waskul, Dennis D., ed. *Net.SeXXX: Readings On Sex, Pornography, And The Internet*. New York: Peter Lang Publishing, 2004.

Williams, Linda. *Hard Core: Power, Pleasure, and the "Frenzy of the Visible."* Berkeley: University of California Press, 1989.

Industry and Workers

Chapkis, Wendy. *Live Sex Acts: Women Performing Erotic Labour*. London: Cassell, 1997.

Jennings, David. *Skinflicks: The Inside Story of the X-Rated Video Industry*. Bloomington, IN: 1st Books Library, 2000.

Lane III, Frederick S. *Obscene Profits: The Entrepreneurs of Pornography in the Cyber Age*. New York: Routledge, 2000.

Milne, Carly. *Naked Ambition: Women Who Are Changing Pornography*. New York: Carroll & Graf, 2005.

Censorship

DeGrazia, Edward. *Girls Lean Back Everywhere: The Law of Obscenity and the Assault on Genius*. New York: Random House, 1992.

Heins, Marjorie. *Not in Front of the Children: "Indecency," Censorship, and the Innocence of Youth*. New York: Hill and Wang, 2001.

Strossen, Nadine. *Defending Pornography: Free Speech, Sex, and the Fight for Women's Rights*. New York: Scribner, 1995.

Effects

Donnerstein, E. et al. *The Question of Pornography: Research Findings and Policy Implications*. New York: Free Press, 1987.

Lederer, Laura, ed. *Take Back the Night: Women on Pornography*. New York: William Morrow, 1980.

MacKinnon, Catherine A. *Only Words*. Cambridge, MA: Harvard University Press, 1993.

McElroy, Wendy. *XXX: A Woman's Right to Pornography*. New York: St. Martin's Press, 1995.

Index